Praise for Leah Vincent's

Cut Me Loose

"Wrenching . . . Her book should be read, not just as a warning of the very real dangers of the world, but also of the price to be paid when, in the name of religion, people forget humanity."

—*The Wall Street Journal*

"A sometimes-sweet, sometimes-harrowing memoir by a smart, passionate, ultra-Orthodox girl. . . . Engrossing and so thoughtfully written, and never mocks the traditions and values of a culture that few of us can fully comprehend."

—People.com

"Painfully raw."

—Susannah Cahalan, *New York Post*

"Gripping . . . Readers will appreciate Vincent's uncensored honesty in sharing the horrors of her past."

—*The Washington Post*

"As thoughtful and heroic as it is gripping and tragic . . . Riveting and relatable . . . [Vincent] familiarizes, rather than exoticizes, the life she's led. . . . The finest example of this sort of memoir yet."

—*Flavorwire*

"Visceral and uplifting."

—*The Daily Beast*

"Compulsively readable."

—*Bookpage*

"Of all the ex-Orthodox memoirists thus far, it is Vincent who best portrays the lingering doubt that lies at the heart of the OTD experience. . . . Serious and sincere."

—*The Jewish Daily Forward*

"The book is not just for people cast out of fundamentalist sects. It will resonate with all the proverbial black sheep who feel pressure to align with others' expectations instead of embracing who they are at heart."

—*The Roanoke Times*

find her voice. The voice Vincent has claimed is unflinchingly honest and incisive. It has already begun to resound on behalf of others who struggle to escape abuse and oppression."

—Anouk Markovits, author of *I Am Forbidden*

"Vincent's writing brims with tension, insight, and longing. This quickly paced book is not about sex, though sex is a part of the narrative. It's ultimately a meditation on love and its myriad cruelties, as well as its eventual beauty and transcendence."

—Margaux Fragoso, author of *Tiger, Tiger*

"Leah Vincent shares a harrowing journey that will speak to all children fleeing intolerance, who struggle to be seen and accepted on their own terms." —Julie Metz, bestselling author of *Perfection*

about the author

Leah Vincent is the author of *Cut Me Loose* and *Legends of the Talmud*. Her writing has appeared in *The New York Times*, *Salon*, *The Daily Beast*, and *The Jewish Daily Forward*. Named to the Forward 50 and to *The Jewish Week*'s 36 Under 36, she has participated in numerous initiatives championing women's voices and the right to a self-determined life. Vincent earned a master's in public policy at the Harvard Kennedy School as a Pforzheimer Fellow. She lives with her daughter in New York City.

leah vincent

cut me loose

SIN AND SALVATION AFTER MY

ULTRA-ORTHODOX GIRLHOOD

Penguin Books

This memoir, which explores one narrative thread from a vibrant life, is based on my memories and my diaries and verified with others' recollections. Names and identifying details have been altered. The character of Deena is an amalgam of a few of my siblings. Some events have been compressed or rearranged in time to more concisely convey my experience. As a girl, I was always told there was only one truth—and it was never mine. Now, as a woman, I know that there is no single truth. We can only convey the raw and awkward shape of reality as we each experience it. That has been my labor here.

PENGUIN BOOKS
An imprint of Penguin Random House LLC
375 Hudson Street
New York, New York 10014
penguin.com

First published in the United States of America by Nan A. Talese / Doubleday,
a division of Random House LLC, 2014
Published with a new afterword in Penguin Books 2015

THE LIBRARY OF CONGRESS HAS CATALOGED THE HARDCOVER EDITION AS FOLLOWS:
Vincent, Leah.
Cut me loose : sin and salvation after my ultra-Orthodox girlhood / Leah
Vincent. —First edition.
pages cm
ISBN 978-0-385-53809-1 (hc.)
ISBN 978-0-14-312741-3 (pbk.)
1. Vincent, Leah. 2. Jewish women—New York (State)—New York—
Biography. 3. Ultra-Orthodox Jews—New York (State)—New York—
Biography. I. Title.
E184.37.V56A3 2014
305.892'4082—dc23
2013016764

Printed in the United States of America
1 3 5 7 9 10 8 6 4 2

Penguin is committed to publishing works of quality and integrity. In that spirit, we are proud to offer this book to our readers; however, the story, the experiences, and the words are the author's alone.

With gratitude to Phineas

and for Leahchke as promised

author's note

Orthodox Jews can be roughly divided into three groups: (1) the "Hasidic," who are mystical and loyal to popelike rebbes; (2) the "Modern Orthodox," semiassimilated into modern life; and (3) the "Yeshivish," committed to the centrality of the yeshivas— study halls where men ponder ancient legal texts. No strong statistics exist on these rapidly growing communities, but a very rough estimate might tally close to 1 million Hasidic Jews, about 1 million Modern Orthodox Jews, and 500,000 Yeshivish Jews, globally. The Hasidic and Yeshivish are the more powerful in the world at large, voting in blocs and lobbying hard to promote their values.

Growing up in a Yeshivish home, I was taught that Yeshivish Judaism was the authentic version of our religion, unchanged since Abraham. In fact, Yeshivish life was invented by my father and his peers. It was a fabricated mask superimposed over an existing religious community. It is not a natural incarnation of religious Judaism, a vibrant, diverse, and evolving faith.

My father and other American Jewish children of the 1950s were raised on stories of their European cousins being rounded up and murdered by the Nazis. For some, these cultural nightmares became motivation to prove their worth, fueling their ascent into the highest reaches of secular society. Others turned away from the opening vistas of the American dream to commit to a stiff reenactment of pre-Holocaust Eastern European life. In ever-distorted echoes, the shtetls' provincial separation of the sexes was interpreted as a strict apartheid. The old respect for the indigent student became a worshipping of scholarly life. A love of tradition became an obsession with the law. This is the way it always was, insisted this new group, who would come to be called the ultra-Orthodox or Yeshivish. The remnants of the Orthodox Jewish community, reeling in the aftermath of the Holocaust, did not argue. And so the Yeshivish developed a story line that extended into the past, as if this way of life had always existed, and pushed forward into the future, as if it always must exist, unchanged.

If a Yeshivish Jew questions his or her path, it is more than a personal upheaval—a break with character threatens the whole tableau.

cut me loose

chapter one

MY FATHER, RABBI SHAUL KAPLAN, was a short, stiff-shouldered man with flat, sad eyes and a high forehead that faded into a bald pate. Like all Yeshivish men, he dressed in a dark suit, white shirt, and black fedora. When we picked through the laundry heap, looking for clean underwear, we would find his sleeveless undershirts and his worn boxers, translucent from too many washes.

There were eventually eleven of us: Goldy, Shaindy, Elisha, Chumi, me, Deena, Mordy, Boorie Tzvi, Dov, Yanky, Miriam. We were each two years apart. We had big brown eyes, olive skin, pixie chins, and wildly distinct personalities.

We called our father "Tatte." Because we were Yeshivish, we didn't speak a fluent Yiddish, like the Hasidim did, but our English was sprinkled with a few words in that language, when English could not do justice to a concept.

My father had called his own father "Dad," but as a child I was not critical enough to reflect on the discrepancy between the little I knew of his history and his insistence that our way of life had always been as it was.

Our three-story home sat on the bottom of a hilly street in a quiet, residential area of Pittsburgh, Pennsylvania. On Thursday morning, a few hours before Passover would begin, I was standing in my favorite spot: behind the open kitchen door, where my mother hung my father's clean shirts that were waiting to be ironed. All of his shirts were white, collared, and button-down, but they were not all the same. Some had a checked pattern of shiny white-on-white thread. Some were transparent with wear. Most, however, had hard stays inserted into the collar, two sharp, oblong pieces of cardboard on either side of the neck. My favorite activity at age nine was to stand behind the open door, right index finger thrust backward in my mouth, sucking hard, left hand on a collar stay. I'd run my thumb and finger around the edge, bend the cardboard, relishing the dig of the pointed end into the fleshy part of my thumb, and flip the stay while it was still in its pocket. My father, busy with prayer, teaching, lecturing, and counseling, was rarely home. As with God, I treasured him through his rare artifacts.

As the ultra-Orthodox rabbi of the largest semi-Orthodox synagogue in western Pennsylvania, my father devoted his life to bringing his congregants closer to God by urging them to leave their Modern Orthodox ways and embrace God's true will: the Yeshivish lifestyle. At this, he was successful. Over the years, congregants exchanged knit kippas for black hats, and delicate hair doilies for heavy wigs.

Our house sat kitty-corner to the synagogue, so in the summer, with the windows of the sanctuary cantilevered ajar and our small bathroom window open, I could hear Kaddish while sitting on the toilet. Whenever this happened, I'd have to clap my hands over my ears. As an observant Jew, you could not hear Kaddish and not respond, "May his great Name be blessed forever and ever," but you also could not speak of God in the bathroom.

Men prayed in the synagogue three times a day, but women went only on Saturday and holiday mornings, and, even then, their attendance was not required. So while my father spoke to God from a cherrywood throne beside the holy ark, overlooking a thousand pews, my mother murmured quick morning prayers hidden behind the kitchen door. I was unusual as a child in that I preferred to sneak away on Friday night to sway along to the songs that welcomed the Shabbos. I loved to feel goose bumps prickle my arms as the languorous "Lecha Dodi" changed halfway into a rollicking tune, almost as much as I loved that moment when the service ended and the room emptied and I could walk through the men's section as if God's home was my own. I would wait on the side as my father put away his holy books and offered some last words of guidance to his congregants. My shy stance declared that I belonged to the rabbi and, therefore, to God.

That morning, before Passover, I stood sucking my finger, fiddling with my father's collars, tucked out of the way, as my two younger brothers chased each other up and down the stairs belting out, "*Tamid tamid tamid tamid tamid b'simcha*," and two of my older sisters had a showdown over a new library book. It was a special day, and not just because of the approaching holiday. This was the day my father went to the video store.

Television and movie theaters were forbidden in our Yeshivish community, but before Passover, my father, an otherwise unyielding man, would relent and rent a few classic movies. They would keep us glued to the borrowed VCR in the attic, freeing my mother to whip together pans of tongue and roasted chickens and brownies and waves of crispy meringues, which she'd ice with thick mocha cream and adorn with strawberry slices.

I sucked my finger until the skin wrinkled, waiting for my father to return from the synagogue.

Please, *HaShem*, I silently prayed to God. Please let Tatte choose me.

When my father finally came home, he headed to the kitchen to talk to my mother. Elisha, my thirteen-year-old brother, home for Passover from his yeshiva in Chicago, bounded in after him, beckoning to me and to my seven-year-old sister, Deena, to join him in the hallway.

"Guess what!" Elisha whispered. Deena and I huddled in. "You're not going to believe this! The butcher, he—he—" With our attention captured, Elisha paused dramatically to fix his yarmulke, which was sliding off his curly hair. Deena and I glanced curiously at each other.

A week before, just after Elisha had arrived home, he had passed on the juicy information that the butcher, a man as tall as a door and fat, too, had yelled at my father in the synagogue, angry about some ruling my father had made. Because he got to hang out with the men, Elisha always overheard the best gossip. We all agreed that the butcher must be crazy. Most of my father's congregants worshipped him, sometimes speaking to him in the third person and always using a tone of respect.

"The butcher," Elisha continued, his eyes wide, looking from Deena to me and back to Deena. "His wife found him dead, completely, totally, absolutely naked on their bathroom floor. The butcher is dead."

Elisha grinned, nodding his head slowly. In shocked silence, Deena and I pondered the strength of God's swift and brutal judgment on my father's behalf.

My father passed us, and the three of us guiltily drifted apart. He reached for his hat, which was resting on a mountain of books. I scanned his face, looking for some sign of God's mighty anger in his features, but my father's eyes were peaceful, his calm lips buried in the hairs of his beard.

"Who do you want me to take, Mamme?" he called to my mother as he adjusted his hat.

The video store! I had forgotten!

Elisha, Deena, and I sidled up to him, our eyes silently begging: *Please, pick me.* Even in our desperation, we didn't get too close to my father.

"Pick whoever," my mother answered. Streaks of blood ran over her hands as she removed the innards from the chickens piled before her. She rested her pregnant belly against the countertop, swiping at her cheek with her shoulder.

"Leah, do you want to come?" my father asked. "You're ready?"

I nodded. My throat was too thick with pride to answer.

"Get good ones this time!" Deena instructed. "Tatte's favorite!" she added accusingly, in a hiss.

"Get the Abbott and Costello with the bases!" Elisha commanded.

Their requests floated past me as I stumbled to catch up with my father, who was striding toward the station wagon.

At Sun Video, I stared longingly at the forbidden pinks and purples of the new Disney blockbusters while my father asked me if I wanted an Abbott and Costello comedy or *Kidnapped*. I did not know that my father had grown up on these classic movies. I only knew that the more modern a thing, the more promiscuous, the more suspect. Non-Jews believed that they were descended from monkeys and so every generation forward was better than the last, but we knew that our ancestors had received the Torah from God, so every new generation was reduced in holiness.

"*Kidnapped*," I told him.

A few hours later, I met Davie on-screen. A brave Scottish boy, he raced over the highlands escaping the bad guys, who marched ominously down the hills. Maybe it was his relentless courage. Maybe it was his blond curls and square jaw. Maybe it was just the right boy at the right time. It was instant love.

My mother stopped by my bed that night, as she always did, her pregnant body sinking into the mattress. Every year of my childhood, she was either pregnant or nursing a new baby.

"Did you say Shema?" she asked.

"Yes."

"Well then, close your eyes and say good night. Sleep tight. I loo loo, Leah, I loo loo." She brushed her cool fingers down the side of my face.

"Loo loo," a child's attempt at the words "love you," was the only way that sentiment was expressed between mortals in our house. My parents were not literate in the language of human emotion. Love was gleaned from the tone of my mother's voice or the softness of her eyes. When I was very young, she and my father would sometimes call me "Leahchke," and there were volumes of affection to sustain me in that generous diminutive. My father was more effusive. Every Friday night, after blessing the children, he would place one careful kiss on the top of each of our heads. Sometimes, as rarely and spontaneously as a sun shower, he would pause behind my chair and gift my head with an unearned kiss.

After my mother left my bedroom, I nestled into my pillowcase, with its smell of sweat and honey, fantasizing: It was my eighteenth birthday. A knock at the door. In came the movie star Davie, dressed in a black hat and dark suit.

"I'm Jewish," he tells my father. "I became religious, and I've spent the past ten years studying the Torah day and night, and now I want to marry your daughter Leah."

I would never be allowed to marry a lowly returnee to Judaism, but in my fantasy, Davie's lineage didn't matter. The sleeves of my wedding dress would be as big as basketballs. "You look gorgeous," everyone would say. In the years that followed, Davie would love me, Leah Kaplan, the way I loved only God: more than anyone in the world, forever and always.

chapter two

THERE WERE FEW PROSPECTS IN PITTSBURGH for a Yeshivish
teenager approaching the age of marriage, so at sixteen, my old-
est sister, Goldy, dropped out of high school to go to the prestigious Manchester Seminary, in England. While Pittsburgh had
a few hundred Modern Orthodox Jews, a few dozen Lubavitch
Hasidic families, and about fifteen Yeshivish families, Manchester had enough Yeshivish people to fill multiple schools and dozens of synagogues. Its seminary attracted hundreds of top
Yeshivish girls from all over the world. Because England offered
an abbreviated high school system, the seminary enrolled girls
as young as sixteen. The sooner in, the quicker out, the faster a
girl could move from her father's home to her husband's.

A few weeks after Goldy left, we leaned our curly heads
around the tape recorder, shouting hellos to her in England.
When she came home for Passover, we ran through the airport
to meet her. "Bazooka gum is kosher!" Deena shrieked, reaching Goldy first, exploding with excitement at this recent piece
of good news.

I wanted to be that missed. I made up my mind that I
would do exactly what Goldy had done. When I was sixteen, I,
too, would go to Manchester Seminary, and hopefully I would
be as successful as she soon was: a marriage shortly after she
graduated and a baby each following year.

Initially, my parents supported my plan, but as my adolescence unfolded, they changed their tune.

The first problem arose when I objected to my father's use of the word *shvartze*.

"'African American,' please," I begged.

"*Shvartze* just means 'black'," he chided me. "Blacks aren't like other non-Jews. They live like animals." His understanding of God's will was vastly different from that of his own father, a rabbi who had marched with black preachers in the 1960s, demanding civil rights.

Then there was the issue of several new brothers-in-law, who wrapped my father in conversations in Hebrew and Aramaic that I, as a girl, could not understand. I was used to my father sharing his wisdom in English at the Shabbos table, meeting my eyes whenever he spoke.

Now my brothers-in-law sat beside my father at holiday meals. "Can you repeat that in English?" I would ask loudly from the end of the table. My sisters rolled their eyes at my immodesty.

"Someone wants attention," Deena frequently snickered.

Concerned about the corrupting influence of my classmates in Pittsburgh, my parents decided that I would leave Pennsylvania a year earlier than we had originally planned. After tenth grade I would move in with my Aunt Fraidy and Uncle Vrumi in Manchester, where I would attend the stringent local Bais Yaakov high school. And then I'd be back on course: Manchester Seminary, marriage, children, grandchildren, the World to Come.

When it was time to leave for the bus that would take me to the airport in New York, I ran after my suitcase as I slid it down the stairs. My mother wagged a black snow cap in my face as I kneeled to tie my sneakers. "You have to wear this hat!" she insisted. "I'll be too worried about you traveling alone. I don't want anyone starting trouble with you."

"It's an old lady's hat!" I grabbed my suitcase and tugged it to the door, where my father was waiting, keys in hand. I hoped that if I could get the suitcase out to the porch, my mother would give up on the hat and focus on saying good-bye and telling me how much she was going to miss me.

"A hat is not going to make me invisible," I protested. "I won't talk to anyone, I promise, I'll be so *so* safe."

"Just wear it," my father said. "You're not going to be harmed, anyhow. You're friends with black people, aren't you?"

I watched him stride down the driveway to the car, my mouth agape at his insult. I had complained about the racism rampant in Yeshivish communities, but I was not so perverted as to be friends with non-Jews.

A playful wind blew at my ponytail, lifting my hair off my neck. "You better go on," my mother said, finally giving up on the hat. "Have a safe trip."

Manchester was gray and wet. Through a steady cold drizzle, I took in my new neighborhood: a religious suburban enclave of low brick homes and small green lawns. The Manchester Bais Yaakov was housed in a decrepit mansion on the far side of the highway at the edge of town, a twenty-minute walk from the heart of the community. I learned my way around the high school and around my cousins, my shyness cloaking me in nervous silence as I navigated my new surroundings.

Night came early in England, and by December, it was already pitch-dark when Jewish Ethics finished, at five. The school day done, I had my backpack in one hand, coat in the other, as I waited behind the crowd filing out of the classroom.

"Hey, Leah, one sec," Shalamit Kohn called over the noisy chatter and the howling wind shaking the windows in their frames.

I froze. The few times my classmates had called my name

over the past few months, it had usually come with a singsong "teacher's pet!"

"DoyouwannacomeoverforShabboslunch?" Shalamit asked, stuffing three words into the space for one. A tall girl with skin the color of weak tea, she wasn't one of the popular girls; she was a brainiac from one of the few families that straddled the line between Modern Orthodox and Yeshivish ideologies. Still, she was miles above an introverted American transplant in the social hierarchy.

I nodded yes, too many times, my chin wobbling in nervous excitement.

The Kohns lived a few blocks away from my cousins. Their house was dark and warm, the lazy English sun barely penetrating the heavy curtains. That Saturday, Shalamit was wearing a scandalously casual turtleneck, so snug the ridge of her spine lifted the back. Her plaid skirt was much more stylish than mine, puddling on the floor when she stood and flying up in small waves as she walked. She introduced her mother and her two younger sisters, quiet girls with bangs in their eyes. Moments later, Dr. Kohn and her older brother, Naftali, came home from prayers.

"Good Shabbos to you," Naftali said to me. He lounged in a dining room chair, chin up, kippa hanging off his hair like a parachute. Gorgeous eyes, I thought. And those candy-pink lips. Is he actually talking to me, his little sister's classmate? A girl? I hadn't spoken to an unmarried boy who I wasn't related to since I was a kid. Once I'd entered my teens, my future marriage prospects would have been automatically downgraded if I'd been caught talking to a boy.

"G-g-good Shabbos," I managed to stutter back.

Dr. Kohn raced through the blessings for the wine and the bread. Over gefilte fish, Naftali brandished his fork and knife, trying to stir up an argument.

"Women should be allowed to study Talmud," he said, invoking a debate that split the Yeshivish and Modern Orthodox communities.

"Hush." Dr. Kohn shook his head. Though he had a doctorate, he was not as ideologically removed as his son.

"There is no valid reason not to allow it," Naftali insisted.

Dr. Kohn launched into a lengthy refutation, explaining why women could not learn those particular texts. "'A woman's wisdom is only in her spinning wheel,'" he quoted. "The sages say that if a man teaches his daughter Torah, it is as if he teaches her obscenities. A woman's brain cannot handle Talmud." Naftali leaned back in his chair, arms folded, lips curled in amusement as his father continued. "Rav Eliezer says that it is better that the words of the Torah are burned rather than given to women!"

My heart thudded in my chest as I fumbled with my fork. Accepting, at least intellectually, the unyielding limits on women that I had been raised with, I wasn't interested in the argument. I was watching Naftali.

Yeshivish girls were not permitted to talk to boys. We were not allowed even to think of them. Since adolescence had arrived, my desire had roiled within, getting larger in the small container of my skin. My feelings were intensified and distorted in their repression. Nearly every boy I saw became a swoon-worthy Prince Charming.

But I always held back. In Pennsylvania, when Mark Haviv had winked at me on Egret Boulevard, I'd whispered psalms to slow my heartbeat. I was the Yeshivish one. I was the rabbi's daughter. I was the one admonishing my classmates to stop meeting boys behind the bakery. I was the one begging them to forget about some actor named Rad Pitt. I was the one imploring them to turn their hearts and minds to God.

But in Manchester, where there were thousands of Yeshivish Jews, I was no longer God's special emissary. No one was monitoring me as I watched Naftali across the Kohns' Shabbos table.

Naftali turned to Shalamit and me. "What do you think, girls? Want to learn Gemara?"

My fingers went numb. My knife bounced on the table before flying to the carpet. Learn Gemara, I thought, the ancient books of Talmudic law and lore that men studied in yeshiva? I'd learn advanced astrophysics in Cantonese if Naftali wanted me to.

"Don't be stupid," Shalamit spit out, blowing her lips in annoyance. "I have enough on my plate at school."

As I was on my way out, later that afternoon, Naftali said good-bye.

"Good to meet you, Leah." He studied me with his head cocked, kippa sliding off his hair. A fleck of white frosting clung to his lip. "She's a quiet one, isn't she?" he said to his sister.

"I'm not quiet," I managed to squeak out. "I just like listening."

"Well, that's a rare skill," he said. I beamed at his approval.

I did not know anyone my own age who had gone *frei*—literally, free. But I knew what happened to those who did. Sinning might seem like all bright lights and loud music, but being free had all the fun of a crazy carnival Tilt-A-Whirl—you'd be hurling in the gutter in no time. I had heard stories about those who left our Yeshivish community. They wound up drug addicts, prostitutes, or dead.

But I'm not going *frei*, I reassured myself as I scribbled hearts in my diary. I'm not wearing pants. I'm not breaking Shabbos. I'm just having some feelings.

A week later, I returned to the Kohns' for another Friday night meal. I planned to disguise my hunger in a costume of spiritual yearning. *Oh, Naftali, but what about the prohibition on women touching Torah scrolls? Doesn't that point to a firm boundary?* I had rehearsed it all in my head. My mind was troubled. My soul hung in the balance. God would have to excuse me for speaking to a boy.

I wore my other Shabbos outfit, a blue suit. The jacket was tight under my armpits and the stitching on the hem was coming loose, but the material was the same color as Naftali's eyes.

When I got to the Kohns', Naftali was there, along with a guy from his Zionist youth group named Jacob. Jacob's red plaid sweater signaled that he was even less religious than Naftali.

The concentration of testosterone in the room made me giddy. All through the meal I gripped my fork and knife, a smile plastered on my face as I swiveled my head, following Naftali, Jacob, and Dr. Kohn as they talked of Benjamin Netanyahu's policies toward Israeli settlers.

After dinner I was shocked when Shalamit joined the boys in the living room, plopping herself down on the velvet couch.

"Do you want to play cards?" Naftali asked. "Fifty-two pickup!" He laughed, tossing the pack in the air. Shalamit rolled her eyes.

"All right, all right," he said. "Let's play blackjack."

My parents forbade cards, but I was too excited to care. We sat cross-legged on the balding carpet as Jacob and Naftali taught me the game. As Jacob dealt everyone a hand, the boys laughed about people they knew and some football team and their youth group.

"Do—do you go to college also?" I managed to choke out in Jacob's direction after I won my first round.

"I'm finishing sixth form," he said. "I'm thinking about going to yeshiva in Israel next year, defer university."

I felt a stab of triumph. Even a boy as irreligious as Jacob, a boy going to college, was going to go to yeshiva.

"Are *you* going to university?" Naftali asked, dealing out more cards. Both of our hands touched the same card for a single magical moment.

"N-no—" I stammered, jerking my fingers back. "Of course not—we don't believe in"—I stumbled over the British phrasing—"uni—university." *College boys and girls mixed and spent their time studying wasteful and immoral ideas.* I had recited this speech to my classmates back in Pennsylvania many times. Life on this earth was short, and every moment measured, judged, and precious. What person on their deathbed regretted that they had not written one more college paper or work memo? Doing God's will, keeping his commandments, and taking care of one's family was what mattered most. Especially for a woman. The outside world, with its short skirts and wolf-whistling men, demeaned women. What could be more beautiful than the sight of a mother lighting Shabbos candles, her children gathered at her side? College was a distraction, an invitation to a corrupt world that would only belittle a woman and seduce a man.

Naftali shrugged. "I don't see what's wrong with it," he said. "You can go to university and be religious. I do. Of course, you have to be smart enough," he ribbed. "Is she smart enough, Shalamit?"

We giggled.

"Yes, you dummy, she's smart," Shalamit said. I loved how outspoken she was, how quick to defend me.

"You don't want a career?" Jacob asked. "You want to be one of those women pushing a pram with a million babies, jumping when their husband says jump?"

"Jump!" Naftali ordered. From his seated position, Jacob gave himself a wobbly little push off the floor, his eyes rolled back in his head. We all laughed.

What Jacob had described was what I had always wanted more than anything else, but I suddenly felt ashamed of it.

"What about your mother?" Naftali asked. "Do you want to live the life that she's lived? What's she like?"

I had never tried to describe my mother. Like the Shabbos or the sky, Mamme was an immovable force woven into the reality of the world. I didn't know how old she was—my parents kept that information sacred, as part of their distant, godly personas—but I did know that she'd been born in Leeds. Her father had died when she was twelve, and her mother had suffered a nervous breakdown. My mother had come to America for a match, looking to escape gossip about her broken family. My father occasionally retold the story of how, on one of their arranged dates, my mother had insisted that she wasn't hungry, but after he'd dropped her off, he had watched her enter a bakery and devour a sweet pastry. By the time I knew her, my mother was a plump and quiet woman, taciturn when annoyed. She could gaze out the window, big eyes wide, overcome by God's awesomeness in a brilliant sunset, but she could also drag a wailing child up two flights of stairs, her carefully filed long nails digging into their arm.

"Well, she's always busy," I said finally. "She cooks and bakes a lot. And my father works very hard, so she takes care of him."

"So basically," Naftali said, flipping his thumb over the tops of his cards, "she has no sense of self. Her life is about serving her husband and kids."

I thought of my mother rushing from the kitchen to the dining room to serve my father dinner, listening intently and laughing at his jokes. "Ask Tatte," she always told us when we had difficult questions. Once, some women had asked her to give a lecture on being a Jewish woman. She had asked my father to write her speech.

With sudden clarity, I saw how different my mother's life was from the exalted Jewish woman archetype I had been taught about.

"I don't want to be like that," I said.

"That's obvious," Naftali said. "You're asking questions. Hell, you've probably always felt different. Wouldn't you say that you want something different than what you were raised with?"

"When I get older," I told them. "When I get married and I'm away from my parents, I'll figure out how to be more independent."

Naftali dismissed this idea. A married Yeshivish woman had no wiggle room.

He was right. A few years back, Mrs. Blaumberg, one of the few Yeshivish women in Pittsburgh, had started wearing one of those half wigs, her own bangs showing in the front. Upon marriage, Yeshivish women wore wigs and snoods to cover their hair, which instantly became sexual, forbidden to be seen by anyone besides their husbands. The rabbis permitted a married woman to allow an inch or two of hair to show without Heavenly punishment, but that was a leniency for when one's snood accidently slipped back. For Mrs. Blaumberg to show her full bangs was to publically flout the law. Then she started taking acting classes at the Jewish Community Center. The Blaumberg kids were doomed. They'd never be able to marry normal people.

I had always sympathized with the children, but now, sitting on the floor of the Kohns' living room, I realized that Mrs. Blaumberg was just a girl grown up. A girl who may have felt apart from her world but was now trapped in a life she no longer wanted.

Fervently believing in the intellectual inferiority of my sex, I had never tried to develop critical opinions on my own, but now Naftali's voice echoed in my mind.

"University is a devil's playground," my philosophy teacher railed.

Naftali wouldn't think so, I retorted silently.

"The Flenkers brought a television into their home," my uncle murmured to my aunt. "Don't let the girls visit their children."

You're such a small-minded man, I thought. Naftali would never react like that.

"Some of you are wearing socks," my modesty teacher lectured. "I can see flashes of the skin of your calves. You should all be wearing tights! God is sickened by your bare legs."

Well, not Naftali's God, I thought.

In the weeks that followed, I looked forward to seeing Naftali after Shabbos meals at the Kohns' or when we crossed paths in the home's hallways. I noted every time he glanced at me, weighing every word he said as if it were Scripture itself.

Shalamit began to get frustrated by my not-so-subtle hankerings for her brother, so I devised a plan to connect with him without Shalamit knowing.

I wrote a letter, cramming round little words into double rows on each line: *Are there some college degrees that are less problematic, religiously, than others? And what do you think of religious people serving in the Israeli army?*

I slipped him the note one day in the hallway outside Shalamit's bedroom. Naftali took it and folded it in his hand. "Do you need me to reply?" he asked.

I tried not to grin. "Oh, please. Yes. Thank you."

"How will I get my reply to you?"

I hadn't thought that far ahead.

"How about I'll put it under your doormat?" he said.

How romantic, I thought.

Every morning, when I left my cousins' house, I stopped to tie my shoelaces on the front porch, shielding my hand with my stooped body as I rolled back the mat. Naftali didn't reply to all of the letters I slid under his bedroom door, but occasionally there was a white envelope waiting for me.

I pored over his responses, trying to pick out slivers of affection from our philosophical discussions. Would I kiss him, I wondered as I lay in bed. If he lowered his face to mine and took my chin in his hand and closed his eyes and came toward me?

There was a hierarchy of sins: gossip, chutzpah, and anger were wrong but tolerated. Talking to boys was wrong and unforgivable. But they are all sins, I rationalized. I'll never gossip again if Naftali kisses me. I wondered if God might accept that exchange, weigh the severity of forbidden touch against all the transgressions I would *not* commit. Of course, I hoped Naftali would marry me. Despite the fact that he was not Yeshivish. He would fall in love with me, and we would convince my parents to allow the match. Otherwise, I would have to keep my crush a secret for the rest of my life.

• • •

One Sunday afternoon, out for a walk, I glimpsed Naftali farther down the block. After double-checking that there was no one watching, I ran to his side.

"Hello, you."

"Hi, Naftali. How are you?"

"Hunky-dory. You?"

"Fine, *baruch HaShem*."

You've got to seize the moment, I thought. When are you ever going to have an opportunity like this again? I summoned all my courage.

"I really like you," I said. "Would you—would you hold my hand?" My Modern Orthodox classmates back in Pittsburgh had confessed to me that they did this—held hands, kissed, hugged, made out with boys. I hadn't understood the mechanics of the more extreme sins, but I knew how to hold hands.

Naftali raised his eyebrows, jammed his hands into the pockets of his jeans. "You're too young for me, Leah," he said. "And I'm *shomer negiah*."

Shomer negiah. Even though he believed in women's rights and college and the state of Israel, he kept the laws that forbade an unmarried man and woman from touching.

One evening when I was twelve or thirteen, I'd been washing dishes when Uncle Tzuki, my mother's brother who was visiting from Chicago, stopped in the empty kitchen.

"Your walk is *prust*," he said to me. I froze, my hand clutching the plate I was rinsing, the hot water burning my fingers. Uncle Tzuki shook his head, eyes on the floor, long beard wagging. "You need to watch yourself," he said gently and walked away.

Prust? Prust meant "vulgar, slutty." Even the word *prust* had to be dealt with gingerly, like dog poop on your shoe. How could a walk be *prust*? It was one more thing to add to the list.

In shul, I worshipped behind wooden partitions, cut off from the men and the cantor and the rituals of Jewish life. A thousand times my mother had yelled at me for letting my skirt creep up my legs when I sat on the couch. A thousand times I had hushed my singing voice because I might be overheard by a passing boy. Modesty was a thick wall intended to keep a man's monster at bay (women harbored no such creature). I was taught that if I relinquished my reserve for even a second, if the slightest hint of temptation slipped out, any male in my presence would transform into a rapacious barbarian. And here I was, offering my bare hand to a man, giving it to him straight out, and he was turning away.

But I wasn't ready to unravel my world with this loose thread. Instead, I cringed with shame. I must be repulsive, I must be fat, I thought. Maybe I smelled bad.

That Friday night, still smarting from Naftali's rejection, I sat in the Kohns' living room after Shabbos dinner, smiling and chatting as if nothing was wrong. Dr. and Mrs. Kohn went to bed early. The Kohns were not as Yeshivish as my family, so perhaps they saw nothing wrong in my sitting on their couch, late in the evening, talking with their daughter and their son. The hours passed. Shalamit's younger sisters put down their card game in the kitchen and went to sleep. Eventually, Shalamit also went to bed, rolling her eyes at my obvious romantic desperation.

I knew I should leave. Being alone with Naftali while everyone slept was forbidden. But I couldn't relinquish this opportunity. Maybe he regretted having rejected me. Maybe he'd apologize and declare his love.

Naftali had been sitting next to me on the couch, his kippa hanging forward to graze his eyebrows. Suddenly, he swung around and put a pillow in my lap. He lay down on the pillow. The weight of his head sank through the feather innards to press against my thighs.

"You're *shomer negiah*," I yelped. The air sucked out of my lungs.

"We're not touching," he said with a shrug. The movement of his shoulders was a shock across my legs.

Indeed, we were not. The pillow was a barrier between our bodies. I looked down at his eyes, at the five o'clock shadow on his square chin. I ached to kiss him.

"I can see up your nose," he said, bugging his eyes. "I can see all the way up into your brain!" He sat up abruptly and stretched, yawning, bending back till his shirt popped out of his pants. "Good night," he said. "I'm zonked out of my mind." He went upstairs to bed. I headed home to my small, cold room at the top of the stairs in my cousins' house.

That night I couldn't stop feeling the pressure of Naftali's heavy head against my legs. Hours passed, but I couldn't slow my racing heart. I tossed and turned, flipping my pillow over, wrestling with the covers, willing my mind to release me into the dark. As my thoughts began to fragment and stretch with exhaustion, a fear descended on my body.

I dreamed that a bar of soap was forced between my legs, inside me. My thighs, pelvis, and jaw seized as its hard edges violated me. I shook my head, trying to lose the thought, but the vision took hold. The soap approached, pushed, rammed itself in.

While my heart pined for Naftali, my mind mulled over his ideas. Realities that had seemed as unchangeable as the color of grass or the wetness of water were now shifting, morphing, offering up multitudes of possibilities and questions where before there had been only unyielding facts.

"Anything to tell me on your end?" my mother asked during

my regular Thursday night call, after the hellos and pleasantries had been exchanged.

All of my internal confusion bubbled up at her invitation. "I think I want to go to college," I burst out rapidly. My words reverberated in the quiet that followed.

"Excuse me?" my mother finally said, a hard edge in her voice.

"I want to go to college." Repeating it made me believe it a little more.

"I don't think I heard you right, but whatever you said, I don't want to hear such garbage. Please. Enough."

"I'm going to go to college," I shot back, determined now.

"Really, Leah? I don't think so."

"I'm my own person. I can do what I want with my life. I'm gonna go to college if you like it or not! I'll run away if I have to. I don't care."

"Oh, really?" she snapped. "You try to do that and we'll just make a phone call to Dr. Pretsky and have him lock you up in the hospital."

Dr. Pretsky? He was a psychiatrist. I hadn't said I didn't want to be religious. I was only asking to go to college. If I got locked up in a psychiatric hospital, my life would be over. It would be a stain on my reputation that could never be erased.

This was the first hard line. A declaration of a strategy: my parents would not negotiate.

It was a tactical error. If they would have negotiated with me, I would have been satisfied. Perhaps I never would have left my faith.

As I continued to exchange letters with Naftali, my friendship with Shalamit grew. I loved that she was smart but also knew how to have a good time. We took walks around the boys playing soccer in the park, caught up in giggly analysis of how cute some of them were. She spent hours patiently going over a

single math problem with me until I began to see the logic behind the series of numbers. I retold her all of *Macbeth* in modern English. She bravely smuggled me a Michael Jackson
mixtape. It was hard to believe that the high-pitched voice on
the recording was the famous Michael Jackson, but I did love
his assertion that I was not alone.

In May, Shalamit dyed her hair blonde, and my Aunt Fraidy
forbade me from returning to the Kohns. The act of dyeing
one's hair (any color, but especially blond) was scandalous.
Shalamit became toxic.

"You have to watch your influences," my mother reminded
me when I called her to complain. "Would you like to visit Goldy
for the summer, after you graduate? You can do a program before you go on to Manchester Seminary. Find some inspiration."

With Israel so close, I had been trying to convince my parents to let me visit Goldy since I had arrived in England. The
offer of a trip to visit my sister mollified me for the moment.
But after I hung up the phone, my anger returned.

That week's Shabbos was never-ending without my usual visit
to the Kohns. After I'd paced my bedroom for the hundredth
time, the small rebellion boiling within me leapt to life. This
isn't fair, I complained to God. I'm probably never again going
to get to see Naftali! How could you let this happen?

We were like ants running around God's mighty palm. After years of thanking him dozens of times a day for every small
thing, it seemed only natural to now blame him for my trou-
bles. And it was a lot easier to be angry at him than to tend to
my heartbreak over the obvious fact that, even without this
new rule, Naftali was not that into me.

Why should I obey your laws? I railed at God. Everything
I want, you take away from me. Everything that feels good is
forbidden.

Now that I had spoken to a boy, it felt as if every other sin would only pale in comparison. Even the Sabbath no longer seemed to matter. I reached out my arm through the sacred Shabbos air and grabbed my Walkman off the bureau.

There was no strike of thunder. There was no voice shouting down from heaven. There were no shooting bolts of lightning zapping me for violating Shabbos.

Sinking to the floor so that I would be hidden by the bed even if Aunt Fraidy burst through the locked door, I flipped the volume to near mute and pushed the PLAY button.

"How does it feel?" Michael sang. "How does it feel?"

The next time I went downtown, I bought *The Very Best of Don McLean*. The fact that it was an old tape from the seventies alleviated some of my guilt over my first secular music purchase. I memorized every word to the "starry night" song. I was the Vincent he sang about. Nobody was listening to me, either. Nobody loved me.

My favorite music about dying for God and the destruction of the enemies of religious Jews now bored me. I needed bitter words to describe the dull ache in my chest. I needed melancholy melodies to assuage the whiplash of my failed attempt at making new choices. Wrong choices. This world wasn't meant for one as *unusual* as me, I thought, reworking McLean's song in my head as I plodded home from school, kicking pebbles over the concrete sidewalk, glum, even as the reluctant sun finally inched its way beyond the clouds to shine on my head for one brief, tender moment.

chapter three

WHEN I STEPPED OFF THE PLANE, the dark air was as thick and hot as a wool blanket. I could taste the dust of Israel on my tongue.

At sixteen years old I had spent eleven years studying the Bible, but I still found it hard to decipher the harsh and rapid Hebrew of the customs officials. My Hebrew was ancient and slow. Theirs had the sharp sound of a living language.

On the curb, men with leathery skin and body hair sprouting from their shirts beckoned me into their vans.

"Jerusalem? Jerusalem!"

I gave a driver my sister's address, hoisted my suitcase into the back of the van, and climbed inside.

Goldy was a tall woman with hefty limbs. She returned to Pittsburgh with her husband and children every Passover. I had faint memories of her as a teen, stomping around the living room, bellowing Mordechai Ben David songs, one fist a microphone, the other pummeling the air like a man beseeching God for mercy. There had been a rumor that she had a pair of jeans hidden in her room, but I never saw them. It was hard to imagine that the tired mother I encountered now had ever been so outrageous.

After Goldy graduated Manchester Seminary, she moved to New York and began dating. Eli, a stiff and nervous young man from a fine family, was her second match. The two of them sat in hotel lobbies and drank Cokes and ate dinner in a restaurant once or twice. They talked about whatever a young man and woman who have never been allowed to chat with unrelated members of the opposite sex talk about, in deciding, over the course of six or eight or ten chaste dates, whether or not to marry. They held hands for the first time after the glass had been smashed under the chuppah. Six years later, Goldy had three children and a fourth on the way.

My first day in the Holy Land, I woke to a baby crying. I opened my eyes, blinking in the sunlight that poured in through the window, baking the air. Cars honked and shouts rose from the street. Goldy screamed in the next room.

"No! I've told you no a hundred times!"

I found my glasses under my pillow and put them on.

Goldy stood in the tiny kitchen, mixing something in a pot and feeding her sons strips of yellow cheese. Her round face was flushed, and she wore a black snood that made her look much older than twenty-three.

"You're awake," Goldy said. "Welcome to Jerusalem. You slept okay?"

"Mamme! Who's that?" one of my nephews asked, pointing his finger.

"It's your *Tante* Leah—remember we saw her on Passover? Remember I told you last night she was coming to stay with us?"

I smiled at my nephews. They wore white underwear that shined against their brown skin and velvet yarmulkes that covered their nearly shaved scalps. Their side curls were tucked neatly behind their ears.

"Is Eli home?" I asked.

"No, he's in yeshiva," Goldy said. "But call him 'Tatte' around the kids—this one has picked up the *chutzpadik* habit of saying his name, and I don't want to encourage that. Well, you better eat breakfast. Mamme and Tatte want you starting in Bais Esther today, and it's already eight o'clock."

I squeezed onto the bench and made a sandwich from the bread and tuna Goldy slid across the table.

The bread was salty, and my nephews stared at me as I chewed. It seemed that I was still dreaming, sitting in this cramped kitchen, in this foreign country, with these children I barely knew.

In Manchester, I had been homesick for months, but once I met Shalamit and Naftali, the feeling had faded. It came back to me now, that ache in the heart for the green carpet of my childhood, the wooden paneling in my bedroom, the aroma of chicken soup bubbling and challah baking in my mother's kitchen.

"I'm not feeling so well," I said to Goldy. "Maybe I'll stay here and help you today instead of going to school."

"No," Goldy said. "This isn't a vacation."

She drew a map on the back of an envelope, showing me how to get to Bais Esther, then gave me a handful of silver coins and a sandwich and had me get ready for the bus.

Outside, the dry air swelled with the odors of garbage and baking bread. The sun, still low in the domed blue sky, burned hot on my scalp.

In addition to the large families of eight or ten children that helped Yeshivish communities rapidly grow, our way of life expanded by reaching out and bringing the unaffiliated into our fold. An entire network of schools and programs existed to teach irreligious Jews about Yeshivish Judaism. Bais Esther, a seminary for women in their twenties, thirties, and forties who were becoming newly religious, was one of them. A few women from

Pittsburgh had gone to Bais Esther. They tended to be ruddy-skinned hippies who wore peasant skirts and plastic bangles to synagogue. There was a predictable pattern: Inspired by my father's sermons, they stretched annual Yom Kippur services into weekly attendance. Eventually, when modest blouses replaced short-sleeved T-shirts and technicalities about making their kitchens kosher replaced questions about God, my father would encourage them to spend a year at Bais Esther to improve their knowledge of Hebrew and the basics of Judaism. They'd return to Pennsylvania with shining eyes, throats hairy with the guttural *ch* sound they had mastered and yielded proudly in their triumphant blessings. To our ears, the ancient words seemed to fall from their tongues like bricks off the back of a truck.

My mother had wanted me to spend the summer at an inspiring program, and Bais Esther had seemed like a good fit. Of course, the slightest deviation from the normal path of high school to standard seminary to marriage market was enough to set tongues flying and matchmakers running, but no one would have to know that I was at such an unconventional place for a few weeks. And if people found out, the fact that I was going to the prestigious Manchester Seminary in September would offset any suspicion about my character.

After a thirty-minute bus ride, I arrived at Bais Esther's campus. The receptionist at the front desk of the administrative building ushered me into the head rabbi's office, a room that smelled of still air and old pages. He was a small man, no taller than me, with a blond beard and a large, thin nose that spread into bulbous nostrils.

"Rabbi Kaplan's daughter, yes?"

I nodded, my throat suddenly dry.

"Have a seat."

His desk shimmered as my head whirled with the stillness

of sitting after the frantic traveling and movement of the past few days.

"I'm Rabbi Mandel," he said, resting his arms on the desk, staring into my eyes. "Your father asked me to accept you here for the summer. Although, as you know, you are a great deal younger than most of the women who come to our programs, and you have a far more solid background than most of them." He fell silent, then raised his eyebrows. "I hear you are going to Manchester Seminary in the fall. Well done. Very respectable. You're eighteen? Nineteen?"

"Sixteen," I whispered.

He tugged the straggly ends of his beard and readjusted his yarmulke. I could feel the sweat dampening my armpits as I imagined him telling me to leave, sending me out into the Jerusalem morning with nowhere to go. I was already on thin ice with my parents. If I messed up this conversation with Rabbi Mandel and even a place as basic as Bais Esther wouldn't accept me, I would be in real trouble.

"Well then, Miss Kaplan," he finally said. "You are very young, but it's only for a few weeks, and I do respect your father a great deal. He is truly a learned scholar. Let's put you in the advanced course—it should be appropriate for your level of knowledge."

I started class that morning, slipping into the back of a room filled with older women. Most of them leaned forward in their folding chairs, their eyes fixed on the tall rabbi resting his forearms on a lectern at the front of the room.

"And now we will examine," the rabbi said, running his fingers through his beard, "the next set of flaws in the theory of evolution, beginning with the fact that even Darwin himself believed in the existence of God."

When the lecture finished, study hall began. I was partnered with a blonde woman named Carrie who had a lazy eye that swam away from her nose.

"You just get here?" she asked in a thick Australian accent.

I nodded, trying not to stare at Carrie's eyes, which seemed to belong to two different people.

"It's such a sensational place, yeah, you're going to love it," Carrie said.

I struggled through the small black letters of the Hebrew texts, trying to suppress my yawns, trying to remember not to gape at Carrie's untethered eye when she talked.

Goldy thrust the screaming baby at me as soon as I walked into the apartment that evening.

"Tatte's coming home any minute," she said. "I have to finish bathing the kids, so calm the baby down."

Tatte! My jet-lagged brain jumped. Tatte's here? The hope that my father would swoop down like the Messiah and rescue me from my life was an ill-conceived fantasy that would not easily die.

With crushing disappointment, I realized that "Tatte" did not mean my father. It meant Eli, my brother-in-law. I shifted the baby over my shoulder, patting her back as I rocked her, weaving my way around the mismatched chairs and boxes of toys that crowded the small dining room. I made my way to the porch, a small slab of gated cement overlooking the street. The baby's breath tickled my neck as the cars below zoomed past at impossible speeds.

My nephews ran from the bathroom wrapped in towels, giggling and shrieking. When they saw me, they fell silent.

"It's Tante Leah, remember her?" Goldy said, pushing at their backs, a pile of towels balanced over her shoulder.

We were putting the children to bed when Eli came home.

"Say Shema with the kids and get them to sleep," Goldy told me, heaving herself off the mattress. As the children clambered into their beds, Goldy and Eli's voices carried through the open door.

"What's for dinner?"

"Chicken. I just need to put it in the oven, just give me a minute, I'm sorry."

"It's not ready yet?"

"No, I'm sorry. Okay? I'm sorry."

"Look at this place."

"I tried. I cleaned up. The kids are always making a mess. And now Leah's here, too. I had to help her out. There's too much going on."

I cringed, eavesdropping on their argument. I wished I could fold my body up into a tiny little form, like the origami shapes I used to make with Shabbos napkins.

My parents never fought. My mother always did as my father said. Only once could I remember overhearing him berate her in a hiss, for not smiling at the guests during the Shabbos meal. I did not know that Yeshivish couples could have as much disharmony as Goldy and Eli did. Of course, secular people who dated casually and kissed before marriage ended up bored with each other and at odds. But my sister had met her husband through the matchmaking system and had followed the rules—I couldn't understand why her marriage wasn't automatically saturated with joy and love.

"Did you pick up that package from my mother?" Eli asked.

"Oh. I forgot. I'm sorry. Okay? I'm sorry."

"Unbelievable. This is unbelievable."

The days passed.

When I got home from Bais Esther each afternoon, I helped Goldy with the children. When Eli came back from yeshiva at night, he snapped at his wife for the mess in the house, for the kids' misbehavior, for having neglected an errand. Goldy whined, whimpered, and stormed off to their bedroom. I hid behind my nephews and niece, avoiding my brother-in-law and his downcast eyes as he tried to minimize any contact between the two of us.

Was this, I wondered, the gorgeous, idealized union I had

longed for all of my life? Was this going to be my "reward" for suppressing my hormonal hungers?

"Eli bought you a gift," Goldy told me a week or two after I'd arrived in Israel. She handed over a book as thick as an encyclopedia. It was a long list of modesty laws. "It would be good for you to read it," Goldy said. "It'll help you improve."

I had lectured my classmates on the laws often enough back in Pittsburgh: Top button closed so the collarbone is covered. Sleeves at least as far down as the elbows, skirts below the knee. Apparently, I had missed a few details.

The book informed me that red, yellow, and purple garments were all immodest. White sneakers were forbidden. Patterned tights were highly provocative. Excessively wide belts were slutty.

I thanked my brother-in-law, but I didn't finish the book. I still saw myself as a fervently observant Jew, but I no longer believed that every Yeshivish rabbi's ruling was an authentic expression of God's will. Having heard Naftali's perspective and having seen my sister's marriage, I had too many unanswered questions. I wanted desperately to be "normal" and believe as my parents and sister did, but I could not smooth over what had come undone.

As the summer dragged on, I poured out my confusion in letters to Shalamit. Goldy gave me envelopes and stamps, and Eli mailed my letters to Manchester on his way to yeshiva, along with Goldy's mail.

I wrote almost daily, page after page, but I never heard back.

My childhood ended over the course of two phone calls, a few weeks apart. The first came on an ordinary Sunday evening in August. I was changing my niece's diaper on a towel on the couch when the phone rang.

"It's for you," Goldy shouted from the kitchen. "Aunt Fraidy!"

When I had left my mother's sister's house in Manchester to spend the summer in Israel, it had been on cool terms. My Aunt Fraidy was not thrilled that her American niece had turned out to be moody, prickly, private, and harboring a growing rebellion. I had been glad to leave her home, knowing that when I returned to England at the end of August, it would be to the autonomy of the seminary dorms.

"Leah?"

"Yes?"

"We just received a call from Dr. and Mrs. Kohn."

My heart stopped. Had something happened to Shalamit? Was that why I hadn't heard from her? But no; there was a cold fury in Aunt Fraidy's tone that seemed to ice the telephone receiver in my hand.

"Mrs. Kohn was cleaning the house, and she found some papers she thought we should know about."

Aunt Fraidy paused. Papers? I thought. What papers?

"Your letters," Aunt Fraidy said. "To her son. Naftali."

There was a tightening in my chest. It was hard to breathe. I had bared my soul in those letters, asking Naftali my most difficult spiritual questions and revealing, in my eager interrogation of his favorite holidays and hobbies and music, my unabashed interest in him. I felt like my clothing was being ripped off in public. The letters were private, a personal risk that I knew might be punished by God, but no one else. Jewish law forbade reading other people's letters. It was humiliating to be so exposed. It was infuriating to be held accountable for my transgressions by people who were flagrantly breaking the law at the very same time.

"We are flabbergasted, Leah. Writing letters to a boy under our noses? We tried extremely hard to make you feel welcome. What could possibly drive you to carry on so? How do you expect my daughters to get a good match if people know they have a cousin running around with boys? You are poisoning our family's reputation. You'll have to make other plans for next year. We don't want you here, in Manchester, in Manchester Seminary. We can't have our family name associated with a shameful person who does such things." Her voice rose to a high-pitched shriek. "Did you consider the effect of your actions? Did you think about how much shame you would bring to your parents? To us? To all of your family?"

Goldy poked her head around the corner. "What's going on? Is everything all right?"

I dropped the phone and pushed past my sister, heading for the door, for the street, tears streaming down my cheeks.

It felt like a death, to me, the implosion of my future. Gossip spread fast in the Yeshivish community. If my aunt knew about my letters to Naftali, every matchmaker from New York to New Zealand knew about them, too. A girl who talked with boys was inferior to a girl who never had. And even before marriage, I would suffer: I had planned on going to Manchester Seminary my whole life, just like Goldy had. If I couldn't go there, I couldn't go anywhere. All the other seminaries would quickly mine the Yeshivish information network to learn that they didn't want a girl like me.

Like a mouse in a maze, I darted down the narrowing paths before me. I was too panicked, too simple, to stop, to turn and face what chased me, to question it, to challenge it. Hurrying through the winding roads of the Old City, I arrived at the Western Wall. I spread my fingers on the stones, lay my forehead against their cool surface, felt the firm rock absorb the tears on my cheeks.

At the end of that week, on Shabbos afternoon, Eli was in yeshiva and the kids were napping. Goldy, curled up on one side of the couch in an embroidered black velvet Shabbos robe, was flipping the pages of a religious magazine. I sat on the other side, lost in a biography of the famed rabbi of self-improvement, the Chofetz Chaim.

"Want some chocolate cordials?" Goldy asked, offering me a bowl.

Startled, I looked up.

"Oh, sure, thanks." I scooped up a handful of the small chocolate balls. "Yum. Where are they from? Mamme didn't send them to you, did she?"

Our mother was not the type to send care packages of goodies.

"No. I bought them myself, for Shabbos. Good, no?"

"Delicious." I cracked through the candy shell. The liqueur heart splashed on my tongue.

"So why'd you do it?" Goldy blurted out. "Why'd you talk to boys?" I looked down at my book. "What did you do with him? Did you kiss him? I can't believe you would do something like that. Was he good-looking?"

I knew that Goldy had spoken with my aunt and my parents and that everyone knew everything that had happened, but my shameful exposure was still too fresh for me to toss around as juicy gossip.

Goldy was undeterred by my silence. "D'you know," she said, leaning forward with a glance toward her kids' bedroom. "D'you know that there are some girls who do things with girls also? D'you know about that?"

Apparently, news of my letters to Naftali made me some kind of expert in all things shameful in my older sister's eyes.

"I don't really know about that," I said. I had heard of this in passing from my classmates in Pennsylvania. Boys kissing each other. Girls kissing each other. Of course, like many religious children, I had explored the crevices of my body together with a female friend when I was very young, but I did not make the connection between that humiliating secret and the taboo phenomena of premarital sex.

"Well," Goldy said with a shrug. "I guess it's not a total shock that you did this—thing. Maybe it's in your blood."

She knew she had me now.

"What? What do you mean? Why would you say that?"

Goldy raised her eyebrows. "Just saying."

"Come on. What do you mean 'in your blood'?"

"Aunt Lilah." She nodded smugly.

"Who?"

"Aunt Lilah." She spoke in a hushed rush. "You know that picture of Tatte in that old album in the attic, from when he was a kid, sitting on the grass with his arm around someone, and the picture is ripped in two? That's his sister. Lilah. She went *frei*. I only found out about her because when I was really little, Uncle Yerucham said something about her when he thought I wasn't listening."

A secret aunt? Could it be?

As a child, I had often daydreamed that secret people existed. That one day I was going to receive an ivory letter sealed with a spot of red wax. *You are the princess of a small European principality,* it would say. *Your current parents and ten siblings are actors. Your true, loving parents are rushing a private plane to Pennsylvania, to bring you, their heir and only child, home.*

It wasn't a far leap from Messiah, angels, and God to hope that there were invisible people who would rescue me from my sisters' teasing or my loneliness at school and take me to a place where I could unfold and breathe. "You're so pretty," those people would say. "Please, read us your poetry."

I knew it was a silly fantasy. But apparently it was true—or at least partly true. I had a secret aunt.

Goldy could tell me nothing more about this mysterious woman. "Promise without a promise that you will never breathe a word of this," she said.

"Fine," I said. An actual promise was forbidden. "I promise without a promise."

I wonder where she lives, I thought. I wonder if she'd like me. I wonder what she's like.

"Want another cordial?" Goldy asked, offering me the bowl.

"Thanks." I grabbed a few more candies and went back to my book, thinking about my aunt who went *frei*.

chapter four

WITH THE ENTIRE ISLAND OF GREAT BRITAIN closed to me, my mother made some phone calls, leaning on my father's influence, and Bais Esther agreed to accept me for the full year. No regular Yeshivish seminary would take a girl like me, a girl who had written letters to a boy. Three months after arriving in Israel, I moved out of Goldy's apartment and into one of the Bais Esther dorms.

Though I understood that the smallest brush with promiscuity spread around a girl and her family like toxic ink in a fishbowl, my banishment from Manchester was crushing. I was not a loudmouthed slutty girl who laughed at Jewish law. I was a girl who cried real tears over the destruction of the Temples every Tisha B'Av. I was a girl who would never sneak a kosher candy bar that did not carry the extra-strict *cholov Yisroel* certification. I wanted to be good. I was good. I had just been curious.

The morning of the day Yom Kippur would begin, I woke with a start. By then, the nightmares had begun. Dead children and dismembered animals and invisible creatures chased my weaklegged body down endless plains. I had not yet learned that if I stopped and turned to face the monsters, they would melt like ices in the sun.

My hair lay in sticky waves across my forehead. My night-gown was bunched into a knot at my spine. The clock hanging high on the far wall said it was only six o'clock, but I was already sweating. From around the narrow lockers that divided the dorm room I checked on my roommates.

Jennifer, a willowy blonde, was stretched out on her bed like a cadaver, a silky black eye mask obscuring her face. A twenty-four-year-old Texan from an irreligious family, Jennifer spent her days at Bais Esther taking classes back to back, often skipping lunch. Some days she took the same lecture two or three times in a row.

My other roommate, Chani, was curled up on one corner of her mattress. Chani was a thirty-six-year-old woman from Chicago who had left her career as an architect to study at Bais Esther. When Chani wasn't in class, she was lounging on her bed, nose-deep in English books on Jewish philosophy, listening to the radio through headphones clamped around her bobbed hair. They kind of cancel each other out, I often wanted to tell her. Rock 'n' roll and holy books. But I didn't tell her that. I didn't tell my roommates much of anything. Chani had trouble holding eye contact, and Jennifer had responded to my friendly questions with enough contempt that my voice dried up every time she whirled into our room.

It was five weeks into the fall semester, and classes were suspended for the impending High Holiday. The empty hours stretched before me, and a ball of crumpled bills lay in wait on the top shelf of my locker. Eighty shekels. A small fortune. Enough for five slices of pizza, fifteen bus tokens, and a bottle of American shampoo.

"Budget wisely," Goldy had said when she'd given me the envelope of cash our parents had sent. "Mamme and Tatte are trusting you." But later that day, when I got back to my dorm, Jennifer stared from my neck to my shoes and asked me if I had only one blouse. She said "blouse" super slowly, with a wrinkle in her freckled nose. Jennifer's tops had woven logos and were folded in stacks that filled her locker and the two suitcases under her bed. I only had three blouses. One of them had a stain down the front, so the remaining two were in heavy rotation. I told Jennifer I had six versions of the blouse I was wearing, all identical because it was my favorite shirt. My poverty had never bothered me before, but now I saw how Jennifer's clothing clung to her body, how the pastel colors made her skin glow. Every day, Jennifer looked fresh and exciting in a new outfit. My few measly hand-me-downs felt like potato sacks in comparison. I was invisible. A nobody.

But now I had my allowance for the entire month of October.

Twelve hours until Kol Nidre, I thought as I turned to the wall, pulling my skirt on under my nightgown and wiggling into my shirt, careful not to expose any skin as I dressed. With no men around, there was no law against nudity, but modesty had insatiable demands. My teachers had told me many times of the woman who, once married, had never let the walls of her house see a hair on her head. She had merited seven sons. My own mother was very careful about modesty. I had seen silver wisps of hair sliding out from the edges of her scarf in the middle of the night, and her glistening nipple when the baby's head pulled back from her breast, but I had never seen her whole head of hair or her elbows or knees. Modesty was a girl's most important mission. Shielding my body from view was my natural instinct.

I wondered, as I finished dressing, what I was going to say to God when I faced him in the Yom Kippur prayers that evening. I had a lot to account for. My anger. All the times I had spoken back to my parents. My bad attitude. My non-Jewish music. Breaking the Shabbos. Naftali.

But I was not going to think about Naftali. I had decided at the start of the semester that I was going to rehabilitate my image at Bais Esther, pulling myself together, so I'd be ready to combat the rumor mill with shining piety when I was done with the year. I recited my prayers every morning and showed up to my first class ten minutes early. My Michael Jackson and Don McLean tapes were buried in the back of my suitcase. I said my blessings carefully. I was respectful to my mother even when she snapped at me on the phone. I pushed away all thoughts of boys, of longing, of college, of freedom.

I'm just going window-shopping, I thought as I walked through Jerusalem later that morning. I'm just going to enjoy my day off and look around.

The streets were packed with preholiday crowds. Men in black coats jerked aside, side curls swinging, eyes downcast to avoid catching a glimpse of a female form. Strollers snapped at my ankles as women with black scarves fastened tightly around their bald heads rammed their carriages through the swarms of people rushing to complete their shopping before the holiday began.

As I made my way into the heart of downtown, the bills from my locker clenched in my hand, I watched the secular men and women stride around their religious cousins like peacocks in a crowd of pigeons. I tried not to stare at their brown shoulders, their T-shirts snug on their chests, their shorts sliced high on their thighs. A cluster of secular teenage girls, clutching cans of Pepsi and shopping bags in their hands, shrieked in fast-paced Hebrew, laughing and tossing waves of hair over their shoulders. They wore tank tops and jeans, their bodies catching the gaze of every secular and religious man not diligent enough to avoid them. How cheap, I thought. They must not respect their bodies. The judgment popped, preprogrammed, into my head. But in my heart, I envied their power over those men. I envied their visibility.

My money poked against my palm. Pinching my nose, I waded through the stench of gutted fish, releasing my nostrils to inhale the yeasty aroma of bread and cinnamon rugelach that drifted from a bakery around the corner.

At the end of a narrow street, a sheet of windows caught my eye. A huddle of mannequins leaned into each other, floral dresses falling off their plastic shoulders. The display reminded me of the stores in Pittsburgh. Not that I'd gone shopping as a child. Most of our clothing was fished out of garbage bags of hand-me-downs delivered by my father's congregants.

Squeezing the bills a little tighter in my hand, I pushed open the door to the store. A rush of cool air embraced me as I took in the racks of clothing. A single mannequin in black pants and a thin, dark gray sweater stood on a platform in the middle of the shop, encased in a dome of glass.

"Can I help you?" a svelte saleslady asked, peering over cat-eye glasses. Her hair was yanked off her face and secured to her scalp with gel, each frozen strand shining in the store's lights.

"That sweater," I said in my broken Hebrew, pointing to the mannequin. "I am able to wear it?" I didn't know the words for "try it on." I'm just having fun, seeing how it looks, I reassured myself.

"Of course, of course," the saleswoman said. "Follow me." She flicked through a rack at the back of the store, lifted up a sweater the same as the mannequin's, and showed me to a changing room. The velvet drape swished behind me like the curtain on a Torah ark.

I unbuttoned my blouse, watching the mirror. The edges of my bra were gray with wear. My body was pale, but my hands and face had been toasted brown by the Mediterranean sun. My thick, frizzy ponytail fell between my shoulder blades.

I stepped closer to my reflection, peering at my face. Behind my cloudy glasses, shadows rimmed my eyes. I look old, I thought. Not like I'm sixteen. I look beaten down.

Turning away from the mirror, I reached for the sweater, carefully releasing it, one shoulder at a time, from the hanger. It was a simple piece. Charcoal gray, with a crocheted collar, cuffs, and hem. The fabric floated in my hands as I slipped it over my head. The thin cloth kissed my skin.

When I turned around to face the mirror, for the first time in my life, I saw a woman staring back. My spine straightened, my movements slowed; I absorbed my reflection from every angle. The material clung to my breasts, cutting in at my waist, defining adolescent curves that were usually obscured by baggy tops. Although the sweater had a high collar and long sleeves, it was too tight to be truly modest. I looked like a woman in a Kmart catalog. I looked like one of the secular women strutting through the streets. I imagined Jennifer asking me where I'd gotten my sweater, looking me up and down with jealousy instead of scorn.

"How is it?" the saleswoman called. I stepped out.

"Do you think it looks okay?" I hoped the saleswoman would see what I saw.

She put her bony manicured fingers up to her mouth, shaking her head with a burst of Hebrew.

"I'm sorry, what's that?" You look stupid, I thought; she's laughing at you. I clutched the changing room curtain, ready to dash back in and yank off the sweater.

"You look so pretty, so sexy," the saleswoman repeated slowly. "It should be illegal."

"If I give you money now, can I wear? No take off?" I asked eagerly, struggling with my Hebrew.

"No problem."

I scooped up my old blouse with the sweat-stained armpits and handed over my cash, my entire allowance for October. For a moment, I was struck with fear. All of my money gone, in an instant. But then I looked down at the sweater, at the double dip as it outlined my breasts, at the delicate edges on the sleeve, and I smiled. *Pretty. So sexy it should be illegal.*

I stopped at Goldy's that afternoon, before heading back to the dorm.

"Do you like my new sweater?" I asked, goading her. I felt sexy in a way I knew she would secretly envy, even as she judged me.

"Where did you get it from?" she asked, stepping into her kitchen, yanking her housecoat's sleeves up her plump forearms, wiping at the sweat that ran down her neck.

"Downtown." I dropped my voice. Suddenly, I was afraid. Perhaps my apparel was a more significant transgression than I was acknowledging.

My niece cooed from her high chair. I kissed her cheek. She shook her head and hands, sending a river of pea soup onto the kitchen floor. I jumped back to protect my sweater.

"What are you making?" I asked. Now I was worried that Goldy might start yelling at me, kick me out of her house or, worse, do what half my brain, the half that was terrified with the power I was wielding, had anticipated she would do anyhow: pick up the phone and call Pennsylvania.

Goldy slid her turban low over her forehead, pushing her stray hairs back into its grip. I held my breath, waiting for her to burst out, but she only reached for the pan on the counter.

"Here, have some apple kugel. Eat up before the fast starts." She put a piece on a paper plate, a shadow of juice spreading out around the noodles.

The kugel was delicious, the noodles on top crunchy and spiced with cinnamon. I wanted seconds, but I was afraid to stay in Goldy's apartment much longer.

The call came the day after Yom Kippur.

"Leah Kaplan! Phone for Leah Kaplan!" I ran for the pay phone and grabbed the receiver swinging on its cord.

"Leah." It was my mother. Her voice was hard. I tensed and held my breath. I knew that tone.

"Your behavior has become unacceptable," she said. "We give you chance after chance, and you keep on messing up and hurting people. Disappointing people."

"What? What did I do now?"

"Do you hear yourself? Do you hear your chutzpah?"

A sharp rock lodged in my throat. "What are you talking about?" I cried.

"That sweater you bought. That money was not meant to be spent on immodest clothing. What do you think this is? An all-expenses-paid vacation? To enjoy your sins? I don't know why you thought you could try and take advantage of us. We've had enough of this. You are not getting any more allowance. You'll have to figure out how to get by on your own."

"But—" I did not understand. I knew I had pushed a boundary, but her anger seemed excessive.

"You think you're so grown-up? Let's see how grown-up you are. You better straighten yourself out."

I lifted the phone away from my face so she wouldn't hear me crying.

"You better snap out of this!"

"Okay," I whispered, but all I heard was the dial tone. I swayed as I hung up the phone. I felt like I was caught in a garish nightmare, my parents getting stricter and stricter, my petty transgressions ballooning into terrifying sins.

I called my father's office. "Leahchke," I could imagine him saying, the smallest of smiles visible under his beard. I remembered how he would kiss the top of my head, leaving a halo of pride that would keep me glowing the rest of the day.

The phone rang and rang, until the answering machine picked up.

"This is Leah," I said. "Can you call me back, Tatte? Please. I need to talk to you."

The next day I scanned the bulletin board beside the phone. There were no messages with my name. I called my father again.

"It's Leah. Please, I need to talk to you. It's not fair what's happening. Everything that happened. Please call me."

I slammed the phone down hard. I stood, staring at the phone, willing it to ring for me. I dug my fingernails into my thighs through my skirt, as if the stinging pain would somehow get my father to call. I looked over the scraps of paper stuck on the board. "Racie B.: Mom called, sent package yesterday, call her back"; "Jessica F.: Dad called, check is in the mail"; "Rachel C.: Mom and Dad will be arriving on Tues., call back."

I grabbed the receiver and dialed my father's number again.

"This is Leah," I said to his answering machine, unstoppable rage rising within me. "Of course, not that you give a darn. I didn't do anything so wrong. Nothing that deserves being treated like an awful person. I hate you! Why are you doing this to me?"

He didn't call back.

Having spent all of my money on the sweater, when my bar of soap ran out, I washed with just water, waking up at six so I could spend extra time in the shower, rinsing off the Middle Eastern dust and sweat, which accumulated like a second skin.

"Don't expect any more money," Goldy said with a smirk.

The woman in Bais Esther's career office informed me that cleaning paid more than babysitting, so I gratefully accepted a weekly *sponja* job. My client was Mrs. Garfunkle, an elderly American widow with watery eyes.

On my first day on the job, Mrs. Garfunkle sat stiffly on her couch, her hands balled in her lap as I kneeled on the balcony and pushed a wet sponge over a pile of dried pigeon poop. The mess clung stubbornly to the tiles. Frustrated, I tossed the sponge to the side and scraped at the gunk with my ragged nails.

"Can you go over this again?" Mrs. Garfunkle asked, directing me back into the bathroom at one o'clock, after I had finished cleaning her apartment and asked to leave.

"Here," she said, pointing behind the toilet and at the walls of the tub. "It could use another go-round, don't you think, my dear?"

I had no idea what she was talking about. The bathroom had looked completely clean to me before I'd started, and I'd still spent an hour wiping down the toilet and sink with bleach so strong it cracked my fingertips. *Clean*, to me, meant picking clothes up off the floor. I had never cleaned a toilet before.

"Oh, oh," I said, nodding my head as if I suddenly understood. "I see. I'm so sorry. Do you want me to go over it again?"

I tried to focus more the second time around, catching all the corners I had overlooked and wiping down all the ledges and walls. When I was finished, Mrs. Garfunkle handed over one hundred shekels and asked me if I wanted to borrow any of her books. I eagerly selected a novel from her shelf and made my way back to the dorm, money in one hand and book in the other, feeling as rich as a king.

chapter five

IN THE WEEKS AFTER MY MOTHER SLAMMED down the phone, I trudged through school, invisible. The other students, older women who were reveling in their spiritual adventures, seemed to melt into a community. I felt rigid, icy, apart. My classmates were taller than me, more substantial. They strode through the halls with swinging arms, shoulders back, taking up all the space they wanted. They referenced movies I had never seen and music I didn't know, forming quick friendships and filling the dorm kitchen with raucous late-night conversations that I felt I couldn't intrude on. These women had left boyfriends and professions behind. They were high on their newfound religion and the charismatic rabbis who taught it to them. They were not interested in me, a shy teenage girl with messy hair and shapeless clothes, and I did not know how to engage them. I had spent my life as a proselytizer; I did not have the skills to befriend peers, let alone single secular women in their late twenties and thirties. I became so lonely I began to mumble to myself in the shower, my voice hidden behind the splash of the water on the grimy walls. In ninth grade, in Pittsburgh, I had waged a *nivul peh* campaign, reprimanding my classmates for using foul language. But now, three years later, those sequestered words rose from me like bubbles. "Hell," I muttered. "This whole situation is—damn crap. This is so—shit. This is fucking shit!"

CUT ME LOOSE · 47

One Sunday afternoon, a group of women piled into the bedroom next to mine, giggling and shrieking. I should go to the bathroom, I thought. I walked slowly down the hall, hoping someone would invite me to the impromptu party. I walked even more slowly back to my bedroom. The gales of laughter continued. Did I wash my hands? I tried to remember. Maybe I didn't. I went back to the bathroom to wash my hands again. Then to braid my hair in the mirror. Then just to touch the wall with my pinkie and count to ten. Finally, I just stopped in the open doorway.

"Hi," I said.

There were six of them, including my roommate Jennifer. They lounged on the rickety bed with their legs and heads in each other's laps, wearing bright pajama pants under their long skirts, singing some non-Jewish song I didn't know.

Nobody heard me. Nobody looked up.

That evening, I swallowed my pride and used some of my precious phone-card minutes to call Shalamit. I couldn't imagine what I had done to offend her that she had never responded to my letters. Had she gotten in trouble because of the whole Naftali fiasco? Did she have a new friend who she liked so much she'd forgotten about me?

"Leah," Shalamit squealed when she came on the line. "How are you? What on earth is going on?"

"What do you mean?" I asked.

"Why haven't you responded to my letters?"

"Your letters? What are you talking about? I wrote you a million times, but you never wrote back!"

It took a few minutes. Eli had never mailed my letters. Goldy must have hidden the letters Shalamit sent me. My sister was always a busybody, collecting gossip. I could easily see her reading all of our correspondence.

"So what on earth is going on?" Shalamit asked. "Why aren't you back in Manchester for seminary?"

"Oh my gosh," I groaned. "Shalamit, my parents are insane." Talking to a girl my own age, I was able to express my frustration. I knew Shalamit would sympathize.

"That's crazy," she said when I told her about the sweater. "I can't believe your parents had such an extreme reaction. What are you going to do?"

"I have no idea," I said. "Shalamit, everything is such a mess. Everything is out of control. There is nobody I can talk to here. I miss you so, so, so badly."

"You have two minutes remaining," the phone-card operator informed us.

"Oh, I have to tell you," Shalamit said. "Remember Jacob, Naftali's friend? He hung out with us one time at the house?"

I remembered Jacob. The dark, handsome guy who, along with Naftali, had pushed me to think about college.

"He came by a few weeks ago, before he left for Israel. I told him you're in Jerusalem. He told me to give you his number."

Flattered, I grabbed a pen and scribbled it down, seconds before the line cut off.

Jacob and I met up at a coffee shop near the Machane Yehuda Market. He wore an argyle sweater and a small kippa clipped to his head. His skin was darker and his hair was longer than when I'd last seen him, at the Kohns'. We exchanged awkward hellos. Does he think I'm *prust*, I worried, because I called him at his yeshiva?

We got falafel sandwiches and ate them on a bench in the sidewalk, watching the tourists go by. I struggled to keep my soggy pita together so the falafel balls wouldn't spill down my shirt. Tahini dripped over my hand. Jacob caught the sticky stream with his finger. My skin tingled at his forbidden touch. I jerked my hand away.

"Just a li'l bit messy, huh," Jacob said. I laughed too loudly and ducked my head. Man, that gorgeous British accent. I let the sound of his voice flow over me as we struggled to make conversation.

"Hey," Jacob said as we stood to go. "Want to be my girlfriend?"

I nodded, swallowing down the smile that threatened to consume my face. If my parents rejected me because they thought I was a bad girl, then I would be a bad girl. I would get through life just fine without them, with Jacob at my side.

"Okay," he said. "I've got to get back. Do you want to hang out tomorrow?"

I nodded again, poking my glasses up my nose.

Girlfriend. The word, I thought as I walked back to my dormitory, had a dangerous ring. I liked it.

"So there," I sniffed triumphantly at the silent phone, which had not rung for me in weeks.

"So there," I hissed at the bulletin board, which bore no message for me. So there. Jacob's girlfriend.

The next evening, I had my first kiss. Jacob's warm breath smelled like onions as he approached my face. His lips pressed gently against mine. He flicked his fingers through my hair. I was too excited by the glamour of being a girl desired by a boy to let my guilt ruin the moment. That night, I lay in bed smiling, placing my palm over my mouth, over my hair, mimicking his touch, trying to relive its electricity.

"You don't drink enough water," he said the next night, swinging his foot and kicking at the sidewalk.

I had skipped evening class to be with him. Since my seminary was for older women, I had no curfew and no supervision at night. It was easy to slip away. Still, I could just imagine Rabbi Mandel or Rabbi Aziz hiding in the cool shadows, ready to pounce and accuse me of truancy. But every time Jacob looked at me, shivers ran down my spine. He cared about me. Maybe even loved me. I was defenseless before the possibility of love.

"How do you know I don't drink enough water?" I asked.

We were sitting on a bench down the block from his yeshiva. His school was Modern Orthodox, so he didn't have to be afraid of being seen with a girl. He had his guitar in his lap. He seemed distracted, plucking at the strings, staring down the street, his gaze following anyone who passed as his sneaker went back and forth on the sidewalk.

"Your lips are dry," he said.

"I'm sorry." I rolled my lips in and tugged at the flaky skin with my teeth, humiliated. I needed to distract him from my flaws. I needed to conjure up his desire.

"Will—I mean, maybe, could you—would you teach me to, uh, French-kiss?"

Jacob seemed unfazed by my prodigious suggestion. "Later," he said.

I blinked quickly so he wouldn't see my tears.

The next morning, I woke and dressed before my roommates stirred in their beds. The cafeteria was nearly empty. Breakfast was my favorite meal. At lunch and dinner I had to navigate a far more crowded room, choosing a group of women to intrude upon while I sucked my food down, as if my speed might nullify the disturbance.

I prodded the cakey oatmeal with my spoon. I had no appetite. I couldn't stop picturing Jacob. The way he looked at me. The way he always lifted his chin before he talked and cocked his head when he was listening.

Still lost in thought in my first morning class, Mystical Secrets of the Hebrew Alphabet, I twitched when the classroom suddenly erupted in laughter. I had missed the joke Rabbi Aziz had made. I pushed my glasses up my nose and tried to focus.

"So the *aleph*, the first letter of the Hebrew alphabet, has deep kabbalistic meaning," Rabbi Aziz explained, his fingers moving from his yarmulke to his beard and back to his yarmulke as he paced at the front of the classroom. "You can see it visually: the letter *yud,* which represents divinity, is on one side." He drew the letter on the chalkboard. "On the other is a leg, touching the ground, indicating our earthly side. And in between is a diagonal line." He finished drawing the letter. "We are not all angel. We are not all animal. We must be a balance of the two."

I copied the letter א as he drew it. I drew it again and again, fascinated by its symbolism. Angel/animal. God/Jacob. Prayer/kisses. I felt like I was being split in two incompatible parts, but Rabbi Aziz was saying that I could find balance with both. I held the idea in my mind, captivated by the paradox.

When the bell rang for the midmorning break, I grabbed my sweater and notebook and ran. *Leah*—I imagined the way Jacob said my name, with his lilting accent. *Hello, Leah, how's my girlfriend doing?* I reached the pay phone down the block from Bais Esther. I didn't want to use the dorm phone. I needed privacy.

I pulled my phone card from my sock and dialed the number for Jacob's dorm, hunching my shoulders to form a barrier between my excitement and the women trudging down the street, crowds of children clustered at their legs.

"Hello?"

"Hi, can I speak with Jacob Duron please?"

"Yeah," he said, after a pause. "It's me."

"Hi! It's Leah. How are you?"

"Fine. I can't talk. You see, this isn't, uh, I don't want to do this anymore. Let's not see each other anymore."

"What?" The word ripped out of my mouth, loud, almost a shout. "What are you talking about? I don't understand." I put a hand over my other ear to block out the car horns blaring at the crosswalk behind me.

"Listen," he said. "I gotta go. I can't do this."

"Are you breaking up with me? I don't get it. What happened?"

"I gotta go, good-bye. Good luck with everything, okay?"

Jacob hung up the phone. I held the dead receiver to my chest and rested my forehead against the side of the phone booth. He hates you, I thought. You must have done something really stupid. You weren't charming enough. You wore that stupid ponytail.

I called his dorm again.

"Hello," a strange man said when the receiver was lifted, his voice falling from low in his throat.

"Is Jacob there?" I asked, sucking in my tears. I had to make it right. I had to get him to see how much I liked him.

The line went quiet.

"No," the man said after a minute. "He doesn't want to come to the phone."

"Can you tell him it's Leah?" I pleaded. "I really need to talk to him."

I could hear some muffled conversation.

"No," the man said. "He won't come." He hung up the phone.

I made my way through the rest of the lectures that day like a robot, moving from class to class to cafeteria, to class again, my eyes glassy, my limbs heavy and stiff. Only when I got into bed did the feelings overpower me. I clasped my legs to my chest, nightgown stretched around my knees like a cotton fort, my heart raw and miserable.

I wished I could step out of my repulsive body. Not only couldn't I seduce Naftali, I had scared away Jacob as well. All the admonishments about modesty implied that a glimpse of a bare elbow could melt a man into a puddle of helpless desire. But here I was throwing my whole self at these men, and they were just walking away.

I already missed Jacob. I could see the days stretching before me, long hours of sitting in endless classes, empty evenings to waste away. No thrills. No human connection. No attention. Only stiff smiles and little nods when I passed my classmates in the hallway.

• • •

The next morning, I didn't go to class. I trudged back to the pay phone on the street and called Jacob's dorm. The man I'd spoken to the night before picked up.

"Is Jacob Duron there?"

"No," he said. "This is Daniel Schwabel. His friend. Is this Leah?"

"Yes." I rested my head against the phone booth.

"You shouldn't call him." His deep voice was kind. "He said it's over."

"I don't understand."

"Listen," Daniel said. "That's the way it is. Men can be like that."

My crying became audible.

"Hey, listen," Daniel said. "You want to talk? We can hang out and you can get it out of your system, make you feel better."

"Okay." I wiped my nose on the back of my hand.

We arranged to meet that night at a park behind his yeshiva.

The late-autumn wind chilled my nose as I hurried through the streets. I tucked my hair behind my ears, flipping it to one side, then the other. If Daniel thought I was pretty, maybe he'd tell Jacob not to dump me. Am I pretty enough? I wondered. Does this skirt make me look fat? Should I have worn my Shabbos heels? I grabbed my cheeks and pinched them pink until they were sore.

I found Daniel slouched on a bench in the dark, empty park. His legs were spread wide, his shirt open at the neck.

"Leah, right? Schwabel. Daniel Schwabel." He put out a hand. I hesitated, but then I shook it. It felt strange and dangerous, his palm against mine.

Daniel had an angular jaw, dirty-blond hair falling across

his forehead, and eyes that ran slowly over my body. I figured he was twenty-three or twenty-four at least.

"Come sit." He gestured to the bench. I settled on the edge, tucking one foot behind the other, wrapping my arms around my chest.

"I know you're upset," Daniel said. "It's good you came out to talk. There's a lot to learn about life, especially if you don't have a lot of experience." He brought his arm down on the back of the bench behind me. "We all have needs; you can't tie a guy down. Especially Duron—he's a young dude.

"Hey, hey—" He leaned in to cup my quivering chin. "No need to cry. Come here."

He drew me into his arms, against his chest. Swept up in the humiliation of Jacob's rejection, I kept my eyes closed, my head reeling, as I relaxed into Daniel's comforting embrace. I did not yet understand the distinction between a gentleman and a sleazeball.

"That's how it is, babe, that's how it is," he murmured. Soon his cool fingers were slipping up my shirt, under my bra. I lay against him, my skin on fire as his fingers sank into my breasts. The feeling was exquisite, but my mind, shocked at the permissiveness of my body, raced with horror at what I was allowing him to do.

"I could drive a girl crazy," he crooned in my ear. He pulled his hand away and then slid it up my skirt, over my socks, until he reached my knees.

"Now you have a tiger cub in you. I'm a lion," he said, pawing at my thighs. He lifted me to stand in front of him and then stepped behind me and rubbed against me, panting in my ear. I didn't know what he wanted, why he moved like that, but it filled my body with confusing excitement. I couldn't stand the intensity of this unfamiliar feeling.

"Please, please don't," I begged. "Please."

He leaned his sweaty face over my shoulder, catching his breath. His chin dug into my collarbone.

"Here," he said. "Dance with me." He lifted my hand and

stepped away in a neat move. I didn't know how to dance that way. One arm trailed lamely as I struggled to push my breasts back into my bra with the other hand, pulling my sweater into place and adjusting my skirt. My body felt swollen. Seams pressed into my skin, and the unyielding lines of my clothing bunched and strained against my limbs.

"You can't waltz?" Daniel asked in disbelief. I shook my head. I knew circle dances and the steps to "Yidden," a Jewish line dance. I didn't know the moves to secular dances. "Here, here," he said, taking a graceful step. I tottered after him, trying to follow, my cheeks burning with embarrassment. "Now step back—Ooh!" I stumbled over my ankles. My wooden body couldn't follow his direction.

"I need to go home," I told him. "I'm really sorry, but I have to go home."

When I got back to the dorm, I lay in bed shaking as my stomach rolled up into my throat and waves of nausea hit me.

In the morning, I showered in the bathroom stall, stepping over the hair rats that clustered around the drain. I soaped my body, raking my nails over my arms, breasts, behind. It was frightening to realize that part of me had enjoyed Daniel's forbidden touch. That wasn't the kind of girl I was. That wasn't how I saw myself.

When I found a message on the dorm bulletin board saying Daniel had called, I ripped it off and threw it in the garbage. I didn't call him back.

I went to classes. I cleaned homes. My classmates continued to ignore me, and I, them. The dreary winter closed in. At mealtime I crammed my bowl with rice and hard slices of bread. I ate and ate until the pain faded to a dull ache. I gained thirty pounds in four months. My shrinking shirts displayed the fat of my breasts bulging over the cups of my bra. My skirts hugged the rampant swells of my hips. I stopped attending Rabbi Aziz's class, sleeping in instead.

My mother continued to call once a month.

"Everything okay?" she would ask in a firm, no-nonsense voice.

"Yes," I would say.

"Well then," she would say. "Take care, I've got to go."

My father never called.

I rarely saw Goldy. I was not brave enough to confront her about the letters, but I didn't trust her anymore. I spent whole days lying in bed under my scratchy blanket, my mind a blur. In the bathroom, I washed my hands with my eyes half-closed. I didn't want to see the bloated chin and rolling belly of the monster in the mirror.

My seventeenth birthday fell on a Saturday in February. That morning, I woke up before my roommates and grabbed the few coins I had saved, stuffing them into my pocket. The money, forbidden to touch on Shabbos, felt oddly heavy.

If I were home, I would have asked my mother to bake a white cake. My mother's white cake had a spongy texture that collapsed on the tongue and buttery frosting that coated the roof of the mouth, until one suffocated on sweetness. I would have sat bashfully at the kitchen table, listening to everyone sing "Happy Birthday," thinking that I might be baking my own cake next year and sharing it with my husband. But my whole life plan had been disrupted, and I wasn't sure what would happen next.

With the money in my pocket, I hurried off campus, sure that guilt radiated from me, a visible aura of sin. There were no cars in the streets. A man wrapped in an ivory tallis strode ahead of me, rushing to an early prayer service. Hugging myself for warmth, I walked quickly down the empty roads.

I had seen Israeli hitchhikers often enough. They pointed down, running after cars, getting in, driving off. But when I got to the highway that led out of Jerusalem, I waited, shifting from one foot to the other. A car, on Shabbos. Am I bad enough, I wondered. I watched soldiers in their olive uniforms cut the line and men and women smile and hold out their arms, shouting their destinations at the slowing cars.

I am seventeen today—fuck it, I thought. I pushed forward to take my turn in the queue. When a small gray car stopped, I whispered, "Tel Aviv?"

"Yes, yes, we're going to Tel Aviv," the driver said in Hebrew. "Come in, quickly."

"What's in Tel Aviv?" the woman in the passenger seat asked as they sped off. "Family? You a student?"

"I've never been," I told her. "I'm just going to see it." I didn't feel like explaining that it was my birthday, that I was confused and frustrated, that I needed to act out: ride in a car, violate the Shabbos, do something crazy to feel alive.

"Ah, an American," the woman said, catching the accent that kept my Hebrew slow and gentle. "Where you from?" she asked in English.

"Pennsylvania."

"Pennsylvania! I know someone in Pennsylvania! You know Shira Sapperstein maybe? She lives in Harrisburg."

I did not.

We sped north with the morning traffic.

They dropped me near the beach. My bravado shrank as I wandered across the sand, passing couples and families that strode toward the water.

What am I doing here? I thought, holding on to my birthday anger like a hard ball against my chest. And then, nestled between the hotels that faced the ocean, I spotted a McDonald's.

Now I had purpose. I marched toward the glass doors, keeping my eyes straight ahead, wild fears rippling through my mind. What if one of my father's congregants was visiting Tel Aviv and saw me? What if one of the teachers from the seminary was in the area? But still, I kept going, up to the doors. Through them. Into the restaurant. My heart thumped with exhilaration. I was making a choice. I was in control.

I had only a few shekels, but it was enough.

"One cheeseburger," I choked out.

As I waited for my birthday lunch, I imagined the cheese-burger sending my taste buds into a wild frenzy, corrupting them permanently, leaving me with a junkie's craving for more, more, more. I didn't care if it did. If my birthday was not to be marked with blessings and good wishes, then let it be blotched with sin. If my parents wanted to deny their love and approval, I would find happiness in forbidden things.

The cashier slapped the cheeseburger down on my tray. The bun was flat. The fluorescent yellow cheese was draped like a piece of plastic over the thin, grayish patty. I carried the tray to a table and sat. A blessing formed instinctively on my lips. I swallowed it away and took a bite.

The meat was dull and slick with grease. The cheese registered only as a gummy, bland texture on my tongue. The masticated sin slid down my throat.

I thought of my mother's kosher hamburgers: the grilled meat crisp on the outside, the tender insides streaming with juicy flavor.

My heart heavy with regret, I waited until three stars appeared in the night sky, ending Shabbos, before finding the highway to hitchhike home. It wasn't worth it, I thought, tucking away my desires. I didn't know what I was doing. I was better off being obedient. My parents knew best. They were right. Sin was a short-lived pleasure that only caused pain. I needed to stop coming up with stupid ideas. I needed to keep my head down and be good.

Back in the dorm, I found my toothbrush and claimed a sink, using blob after blob of precious American toothpaste to scrub my mouth clean.

chapter six

IN MAY, AFTER I'D FINISHED A YEAR in Jerusalem, my parents arranged for me to move to New York. My sisters Goldy, Shaindy, and Chumi had all lived there between seminary and marriage, and it would raise more red flags if I didn't do the same.

Brooklyn was home to thousands of Yeshivish girls impatiently waiting out the painful limbo between childhood and motherhood. Those who weren't native to the city took up residence in tiny basements and attic apartments, finding jobs as secretaries or schoolteachers, each girl holding her breath as she waited to be picked—by a matchmaker, by a prospective mother-in-law, by a man—so her life could begin.

I'd be married very soon. I was sure of it. Since my seventeenth birthday, in February, my collar had stayed buttoned and I had expanded my usual abbreviated morning Brachos, Shema, and Shemoneh Esrei to the full female version of Shacharis prayers. It was only a matter of months before some tall, good-looking yeshiva boy would be standing beside me under a velvet canopy, holding a gold band between his fingers.

I was thin enough for it. In the last weeks in Israel, as I'd counted down the days until I came back to the States, I had taken long walks, wandering the streets of Jerusalem for hours. I'd avoided the cafeteria, letting hunger growl in my belly until my bras held my breasts securely again and the fat receded from my face.

My mother had kindly made a few phone calls and found me a studio apartment in the basement of a neighbor's cousin's house for $450 a month, as well as a job in midtown Manhattan, as a secretary at Sunshine Bags Inc.

On my first day at work, just before lunch, Shimi Berger, the owner, rushed around the corner toward my desk. Shimi was a smooth-cheeked religious man in his fifties. His carpeted suite of offices was hung with plaques proclaiming his generosity to poor Jewish brides, yeshivas in Israel, the Jewish volunteer EMS service, Sabbath food for the needy, and religious education for poor Russian immigrants.

"Were you not told to hang up the phone after paging?" Shimi asked me. He was a stern and handsome man, with an ample stomach on a burly build. "Were you not told?" he repeated. "It's highly disruptive to the entire office to have to listen to every sound and clink and noise you make."

I opened my mouth, but no words came out.

"Please," he said. "Hang up after you page someone. It's important to remember."

I nodded my head, ponytail bouncing vigorously as he left.

Lakisha, the office manager, strode over, her gold stiletto sandals clicking on the floor.

"Here," she said, her slim brown arms reaching for the phone. "Don't worry about him, honey. Just press HOLD, dial the extension, press the active line, and then press TRANSFER."

I struggled through my first day, my head spinning, my shoulders clenched. My voice was too low for the phone, the filing too complicated, the reports too complex. I was just waiting for Shimi to come rushing around the corner and berate me, then fire me. *I've had enough!* he'd yell. *Get out of here!* Then what? No dinner. No apartment. Another black mark on my reputation. *Oh, Leah, she's a messed-up girl. Wrote letters to a boy. Went to Bais Esther. Can't even hold down a job. I don't know any boys who would be a good match for a* nebech *like her.*

When five o'clock finally arrived, I rode the subway back to Brooklyn, dozing with my head against the scratched window, sneaking bleary glances at my reflection, at my cheekbones, sharper than they'd ever been, at the dark valleys cut under my eyes. I had been in America for six days and the jet lag still had a hold on me.

At Eighteenth Avenue, I trudged past row houses and apartment buildings squeezed side by side. I skirted the abandoned tires, the foam McDonald's shells, and the bags of garbage that had baked all day in the late-spring heat. A man in a car double-parked on the corner leaned on his horn. *Hoooonk*. Kensington, the neighborhood I lived in, was a mix of Yeshivish Jews and black and Hispanic families. It was a poor area, with boxy brick homes, trash-strewn streets, and a bodega on every corner.

My apartment was the size of a walk-in closet. The front door opened up to the bed. A table with a rusty folding chair and a fridge were crammed at the foot of the mattress. The stove and sink were across from the fridge, and the thin walkway in between led to the tiny bathroom. It stunk of mold.

Despite its deficiencies, I loved my new home. It reminded me of the clubhouses I'd built from sheets and chairs when I was a child. It was all mine. There was no one to bother me.

I fell into bed with my clothes and shoes still on. My mind swam with numbers for extensions and passwords. My empty stomach rumbled. My sleep was shallow and unsatisfying. I watched, bleary-eyed, as the sliver of sky outside the narrow window brightened with the morning light.

On Wednesday, there was a heel of bread on the kitchen counter; I ate it for breakfast in two bites. My parents had paid my first month's rent, but beyond that I was expected to manage on my own. I had exchanged the few shekels I had saved for a loaf of bread, a roll of toilet paper, and some subway tokens. I would have to wait until I got paid, on Friday, for anything more. My parents did not coddle any of their children, but they had been more generous to my sisters when they had been single girls living in New York. I felt that they were still punishing me for not being the daughter they'd hoped for.

On Thursday morning, I stood staring into the empty refrigerator for long minutes before easing the door shut. I had a cup of tap water for breakfast. At work, my jaw ached from clenching my teeth as I struggled to remember my duties. Caught up in learning how to use the computer database, I didn't feel my hunger until I got into the elevator at the end of the day.

When I woke on Friday, my stomach was twisted in knots. I stood up and the walls of my apartment swayed. Look how skinny, I thought, running my fingers over the ridges of my ribs, trying to be cheerful.

Before I left the house, I scraped pieces of ice off the walls of the freezer with my nails and sucked on them. At work, I answered the phones and distributed faxes, blinking hard to clear my fuzzy vision.

"Hon, do you want me to take the phones so you can go get lunch?" Lakisha asked at noon. She had done her hair in tiny cornrows that made her look like an African princess.

"No," I told her, swallowing hard to hide a quiver of self-pity. "I need to catch up on things, so I'm not going to lunch today." If I took a break, the hunger would only get bigger.

The office closed early on Fridays, for Shabbos. At two minutes past three, Lakisha handed me an envelope. For two and a half days of work, my check was eighty-five dollars and forty-eight cents.

There was a small storefront on the corner that cashed checks. I stood in the long line, shifting from leg to leg. The back of my throat burned as images of food flashed through my mind. Kokosh cake. Soft kokosh cake with thick chocolate layers, the sugary crumbs melting on my tongue. Chicken thighs, crispy on the outside, buttery on the inside.

Finally, it was my turn. The older man behind the window

took the check from me, pinching it between yellow finger-nails lined with dirt. He looked at the check, looked at me.

"There will be a dollar-fifty fee to cash this check, ma'am."

"Okay, okay."

Slowly he counted out the bills and the change and pushed them forward.

I grabbed the money and ran.

There were no kosher restaurants near work, so I bought a bag of kosher potato chips and a box of cookies from the corner bodega. I stood in the street and ate. Crumbs spewed out of my mouth, my hand zipping a rapid path between the bag and my tongue. The hard edge of a chip scratched against my throat. I sputtered, swallowed hard, gasped, downed another chip. I remembered a teaching from my childhood: one who eats in the street is compared to a dog. Ashamed but still ravenous, I ran my wet finger along the bottom of the bag, catching any last bits and licking them off.

When my parents had sent me a return ticket to America, I'd thought that meant I was being welcomed back into the family. Four months of showing up to seminary classes on time and saying my blessings slowly before and after eating and burying all thoughts of boys had tamed my demeanor and they had been convinced through my teachers' reports that things had gone back to normal. But since my arrival in New York, my mother had remained curt and cold. There were no dropped hints about dating, no mentions of yeshiva boys who might be suitable for me.

My role was to play mild indifference and sweet ignorance, as older women schemed and conjectured. All I could do was wait and fret. It seemed my indiscretions were not being so easily dismissed. I'd thought I was squarely back on the path, but, in truth, I was still in limbo.

• • •

There is little room for the single girl in Yeshivish life. For a woman, the rhythm of observance is tied to family. One is either a daughter or a wife. When my sisters had lived in New York, they'd spent Shabbos and holidays with friends from seminary who had family in New York. My sisters were extroverted girls who attracted new relationships like magnets. I had no friends from seminary, and I was not bold enough to make friends with strangers or approach distant cousins and ask if I could join them for a meal.

The worst part of the loneliness was how it compounded my boredom. Television, of course, was forbidden. I did not belong to a shul; as a girl without a husband or father on the other side of the *mechitza*, I was not expected to attend services. When I got home from work, I ate a slice of pizza or an apple for dinner, said my evening prayers slowly, showered for as long as I could stand, and then lay in bed in my nightgown, baking in the heat, worrying about my future as the moments dragged by.

One night, the boredom and humidity became unbearable. I pulled on a skirt and blouse and walked through the dark streets. The traffic lights blinked at the empty roads. I skittered around the men gathered under plastic bodega awnings on the corners. From the park under the elevated train tracks, I could hear shouts and calls. Eventually, I returned to my crumpled sheets, to watching the low ceiling that hovered above my face. *What's next?* I wondered. *If there is no world of dating and marriage waiting to pull me in, why am I here?*

One Sunday in the beginning of June, I went to the small public library down the block from the subway station; there I found a college reading list on a red cardboard bookmark. I had given up all hope of going to college, but there was nobody to stop me from checking out all the books on that list and devouring them. *The Bluest Eye* and *The Catcher in the Rye* and *The Grapes of Wrath.*

Each day I went through the motions of my job and then counted the long hours of the evening, alone in my apartment. I said the Shema prayer every night before sleep, but heaven seemed unresponsive.

I was always hungry. My minimum-wage check barely covered the rent, the phone bill, and the electric bill. On too many Thursdays I was left with just a slice of bread, a bottle of ketchup, and a few pieces of American cheese. I baked grilled cheese, chewing each piece dozens of times to make it last. I melted cheese and ketchup in a pot on the stove to make a gooey soup, which I choked down. I squeezed the ketchup into circles on my palms and lapped it up. I made a "salad" of bread and cheese and garnished it with ketchup.

In my father's parables, holy men were always scraping together pennies for weddings or Shabbos food. Poverty and spirituality seemed synonymous. As a child, wearing hand-me-down clothing and living with broken furniture just made me feel proud of our family's devotion to God.

But there was no spiritual superiority in mixing hand soap and water in an empty shampoo bottle and hoping the resulting mixture would leave my hair shiny and clean. There was no magic in stuffing ribbons of toilet paper into my socks at work to smuggle home. There was no God in the dry taste of stale bread for breakfast, lunch, and then dinner.

After a few weeks, I picked up the phone and called my mother.

"It's Leah."

"Hello. Hold on—One second, Boorie Tzvi! Everything okay?"

"Yes."

"It's very hectic now. Okay—"

"Mamme," I cut in before my mother could hang up. "Things

are tough. You know. Even with my job, it's hard. I don't always have money for stuff, for food and stuff." My instinct was to hide the choke in my voice, but I let it go. I wanted my mother to see the evidence, to understand how lost and overwhelmed I was feeling. "Could you help me, maybe?"

"Come on," my mother said. "Stop being melodramatic, Leah. It's not like you're starving. You're a grown-up now. You have to learn to stand on your own two feet."

"I know," I said, wiping my eyes on the back of my hand, ashamed of my outburst. "But it is—it is hard. I'm finding it hard."

"We'll see." My mother sighed. "I just don't know what happened. It feels like it's one thing after another with you. You were always such a well-behaved girl. How did you become who you are now? I tell you, sometimes I think you must be possessed by a dybbuk. I don't know how else to explain who you have turned into."

A chorus of shouts rose behind her.

"I've got to go now," she said. "The children need me."

A dybbuk? The diagnosis shocked me. Yeshivish Jews were not quick to speak of mystical things, let alone claim possession by a foreign evil spirit. That was the domain of the Hasidim. It was unsettling to hear my mother borrow such a foreign explanation.

If my mother thought I was possessed, then my prayers and stringencies had been for naught. There would be no thrilling conversations about someone's son or nephew or cousin. There would be no examination of the life of some boy, of the schools and camps he'd attended, friends and neighbors, family, good deeds, personality. A possessed girl. I was marked forever.

A few days later, a twenty-dollar check arrived in the mail. I had hoped for a more robust salvation, but I was grateful for the slice of pizza, jar of peanut butter, bag of apples, bottle of shampoo, and six cans of tuna my mother's money bought.

• • •

The June heat deepened into the unrelenting broil of July. When I wished Lakisha good morning, my voice sounded off-pitch after having not been used since I had left work the day before. I had been a quiet child in a noisy family, a nerdy outcast in high school, a shy teen in a lively women's seminary. I was used to loneliness. But this was different. Masses of New Yorkers swarmed by me on the street and on the subway, as if I were invisible. My emotions built up within me, ricocheting without release.

At lunch, I leaned against Sunshine Bags's building, doling out precious bread crumbs to attract a crowd of pigeons. I was disgusted to realize how joyful I became at the sight of their bobbing silver heads rushing toward me. But as pathetic as I felt, I could not stop throwing my lunch at them. Pigeon friendship, I thought despondently. All I'm left with is the attention of birds.

On the way to the train every morning, I passed a park, a rectangle of asphalt that spanned half a block. At one end was a basketball court, cordoned off with a chain-link fence, behind which black men sprang for the ball, their skin rippling and shining, their shouts cutting through the heat.

It became a habit to stop at the park on my way home from work and watch the basketball game, enviously stalking the jostling men with my eyes, a way to pass the long, hungry hours. Every day, I came and sat. I longed for my stares to beckon one of those vibrant people to the bench where I sat, to look at me, talk to me. But even when they ambled past me to get to the courts, the men gave me only a glance before passing. I lived for those looks, for the brief flash in someone's eyes that proved I existed. A few times I tried wearing the tight gray sweater I had bought in Israel, even though I began to sweat minutes after struggling into it. I hoped that the curves it revealed might elicit more glances, compel someone to talk to me. But it had no effect.

One night, lying in bed, fanning my nightgown over my legs to try to create a breeze, the hours of dark stretching before me, I was hit with an idea, a ticket to the world of those exotic strangers. I switched on the light, grabbed my glasses, pulled out my notebook, and began to write.

The next day, I went to the park after work, notebook in one hand, pen in the other, and settled onto my familiar park bench. I was ready to put my plan into action. But I couldn't find the courage to leave the safety of my seat and walk onto their territory, the court, to bring my idea to life. The next day, the same. The third day I forced myself to approach a large black woman who sat at the edge of the basketball court.

I didn't know any black people, except for Lakisha. Kenny, the custodian in my brothers' elementary school, back home in Pittsburgh, was black, but no one talked to him, although sometimes my brothers would sing, "Kenny, Kenny, he's so smelly, flush him down the toilet bowl!"

The woman let her hazel eyes rove over my low ponytail, glasses, long-sleeved blouse, and ankle-length skirt.

"Yeah," she said.

"Hi." A sticky plug of shyness closed off my throat. I swallowed hard. "I'm doing a survey on happiness and human potential. Can I ask you some questions?"

I had been thinking about my own happiness—specifically, my doubts that only a Yeshivish outlook could lead to a joyful life, as I had been taught. I wondered what other people might think about these things. People as different from my parents as possible.

"A wha'?"

"A survey on happiness and human potential."

"Oh, I'm no good with them things," the woman laughed. "Ask him. Hey, Roadster! This girl wanna ax you some questions for some survey thing."

A bald man in basketball shorts and a net undershirt

strolled over from the side of the court, where he had been chugging down a two-liter bottle of Pepsi.

"What?"

"Hi,I'mdoingasurveyonhappinessandhumanpotential," I said breathlessly. Roadster stared, one eyebrow raised. "Can I ask you some questions?"

"Questions?" He narrowed his eyes. I nodded eagerly. "All right," he said after a second, with a shrug of his shoulders. "But it's gotta be quick, 'cause I gotta get back to the game. Whachu doing this survey for?"

"It's a research project for school." My voice quaked with the lie I had prepared.

"A'ight." Roadster let his eyes wander over my body, then wiped at his sweaty forehead with the bottom of his shirt, revealing waves of muscle across his dark stomach. "What's the questions?"

"Well, what do you do for a living?" I asked, consulting my notes.

"I work at a photo place. In midtown."

"How do you define 'happiness'?"

"Shiiit. What kind a question is that?"

"N-no, I'm—I'm so sorry—" I stammered, worried that I had offended him, that he might walk away and leave me stranded on the court, looking like an idiot. "It's—it's just a survey on happiness and human potential."

He rolled his eyes toward the game, gulping down his Pepsi until the plastic bottle caved under his persistent mouth. A guy grabbed the ball, jumped toward the hoop, dunked the ball. I waited for Roadster to turn back to me, gripping my notebook in my hands, a river of sweat forming where the underwire of my bra cut into my ribs.

"What's the question again, miss?"

"How—how would you say you define happiness?"

"Basketball, or cold soda, a forty. Things, I don't know. Or winning the lottery." I scribbled down his answers, balancing my notebook on my forearm.

"And who—who is your hero?"

He shrugged.

"Don't know. Don't have any, I guess. People are people. Don't got no heroes."

"ROAD-STER," a guy shouted from the game.

He grinned at me, tossed the empty soda bottle on the ground, and took off running for the ball.

I wrote careful notes about the interview, trying to embody how I imagined an academic might sound. *Subject appears to be in late twenties. Question about happiness disoriented him. Lack of cultural appreciation for self-awareness???? Or is happiness taken for granted???*

"Whachu doin', miss?"

A man who had been playing ball sidled up to where I stood on the edge of the court. He was as short as me, with cocoa skin and tight curls cut close to his head.

I laughed nervously.

"My name is Leah—I'm not a miss. Can I ask you some questions for a survey project?"

"Sure."

His name was Coffee. He did nothing for a living, he told me.

"And, who would you say—who is your hero?"

"Your boyfriend," Coffee wisecracked with a cackle, sweeping his eyes down to my breasts, where they stayed.

I smiled nervously, pleased with the attention. After Coffee, I interviewed José and P. J. McDonald and Roy and Doctor Soot and Leon. My interviews gave me an excuse to return to the basketball court, again and again. It became increasingly difficult to go back to my silent bed. I stayed out each night, listening shyly to their conversations, watching the games, enjoying the smoky silences, slipping into my apartment just before the sun stained the sky. After a brief nap, I would spend my tired day counting the minutes until I could go back to the park and sit on the bench and wait for the men to come say hello, to settle beside me with a beer hidden in a paper bag and joke and talk with each other, occasionally throwing a question my way, always slipping their eyes over me, reaching for my hand too, sometimes kissing me on the cheek. Their friendly touches were forbidden, but I couldn't reject them. It was a small price to pay for the pleasure of belonging.

Roadster, the first man I interviewed, became my friend. He lived one block over from me, and we sometimes walked home together.

"You walk like a guy," he told me one night, laughing as we sauntered down the silver path of streetlamp light in the middle of Cortelyou Road.

"What do you mean?"

He showed me, swinging his shoulders like a gangsta. I laughed. I had been mimicking the basketball players, unconsciously.

"Nah," he said. "You gotta walk like the girls. With your hips. You gotta move your hips."

I remembered my Uncle Tzuki telling me, years before, that my walk was slutty. Now, as I watched Roadster demonstrate an exaggerated feminine stride, stumbling and prancing down the street, shaking his hips, I wondered if that's how my uncle had seen me.

Roadster never let his eyes linger too long on my breasts. He acted like he was untouched by the silent desire that swam around me and the other men. I trusted him.

"Why do they tickle my hand when they say hello?" I asked him one night.

"Like this?" He took my hand and ran his fingers over my palm, but without the eye-gripping stare that usually accompanied that greeting. I pulled my arm back. I was still not entirely comfortable with touching a man.

"Yeah."

He laughed. "It's a come-on. They be flirtin' with you."

I turned away so Roadster wouldn't see me swallowing my smile. Later that night, I stripped naked and stood on a chair in the bathroom so I could see my body in the mirror above the sink. *They be flirtin' with you.* I grinned at my reflection as I examined my body, trying to imagine what those non-Jewish men saw when they looked at me.

I never gave Nicholas my survey on happiness and human potential. He didn't come around the park as often as the others, but I noticed him right away. He was in his mid-twenties, with high carved cheekbones and curly hair matted in three clumps of dreadlocks. His words were smeared thick with a Jamaican accent. "What? What's that?" I asked again and again, when we finally got to talking. Nicholas laughed, flashing his prominent teeth. I was embarrassed by my difficulty understanding him, but I kept looking for him, sidling over to wherever he parked himself, offering a timid hello, praying he'd start a conversation. He often sat on a bench by himself, brooding in a powerful, masculine silence.

One warm night, well after midnight, as trains rattled by on the tracks overhead, Nicholas and I straddled the park bench, leaning into each other in earnest conversation. My hair was pulled back in a bun, and I had rolled up the sleeves of my pink blouse to my forearms. I wasn't comfortable exposing my elbows. Nicholas was wearing a baggy T-shirt with the word BIG and a photo of an overweight black man's face on it. His jeans hung so low I could see his plaid boxers.

"So you're a Rastafarian," I asked. "What do you believe? What does that mean?"

He was the only man in the park who seemed devoted to any sort of spirituality. I wondered if I might find something for myself in his beliefs, since the God I knew felt so far away. At the very least, spirituality was one thing I seemed to have in common with this stranger.

"It's Jah's world," Nicholas said. He shifted forward, and his beer bottle fell over my skirt, spilling amber liquid across the cotton pleats. His eyes glinted in the streetlight. His fingers patted at the cloth.

"Ahm sorry, princess. Sorry."

Princess. The way he said it reminded me of my father calling, "Leahchke!" *Leahchke*, like a blessing, the diminutive a gift.

"You okay, princess?"

"Don't worry. No big deal—it's all right." I laughed to reassure him and hurried home to change into a dry skirt, then returned to the park, offering up a prayer of thanks when I found Nicholas still sitting there, a dark statue carved in the dark night. The rest of the park was empty. The surrounding streets were quiet.

"Jah, this Jah, is that the same thing as God?" I asked, swinging a leg over the bench, settling right back into the conversation.

"It's an honor that Nicholas calls you princess," Roadster said with appraising eyes as we walked home together one night. "He wants you."

I shoved him playfully, the light contact of our bodies zapping my skin with chills.

"Stop it," I protested, embarrassed and confused. "You know I don't do anything with guys. It's against my religion."

But late one Thursday evening at the end of July, when Nicholas asked me if I wanted to go somewhere with him, I nodded eagerly. He likes me, I thought, scampering after him. Is he going to kiss me tonight? Is he going to tell me he secretly loves me?

We walked silently. Nicholas wheeled his bike beside him.

Each time we passed a Jewish man hurrying home from evening prayers, I slowed or looked away, as if the tall black man
beside me was a stranger.

A few blocks away from the park, we arrived at an apartment
building. I followed Nicholas as he carried his bike up the stairs.
At the third floor he fumbled with a key and we went inside an
apartment. Goose bumps rose on my arms. Excitement, but not
fear. I was not afraid of strangers that summer. I could not allow
myself to feel afraid. Fear lived only in sleep, in nightmares.

Nicholas led the way through a dark hallway and into an empty
room. He sat down on the floor, his back to the wall. I followed
him, folding my skirt carefully under my legs. The large room
held the sharp odor of pesticide. Light from the streetlamps filtered
through two dusty windows. There was no furniture. As my eyes
adjusted to the dark, I saw scattered cans of paint and pieces of
plywood balanced against the wall. Thumps and muffled voices
filtered into the room from the apartments above and below us.
Nicholas pulled a lumpy rolled-up paper out of his sock and lit it,
sucking deeply on its end. It had an unusual smell, sweet and heavy.

"Is that—is that a cigarette?" I asked, wrapping my arms
around my knees.

He laughed loudly, his teeth shiny in the dark.

"No, princess, it's a spliff. Want some?" He held it out. I
looked from it to him, back at it. "You don't know what a spliff
is?" He clicked his tongue against his teeth. "For real?"

I couldn't tell if I had pleased or annoyed him. I had already
learned that some people found my cultural ignorance charming,
while others were frustrated by it. The trick was knowing which
reaction was coming and adjusting my responses appropriately.

"I don't. What is it?"

"It's ganja. Mar-ee-wah-nah." He pronounced the word like
four separate words. I knew marijuana was a drug. Back home
in Pittsburgh, my classmates had told me about it, but I had
never seen it. I didn't realize that was how it looked.

He sucked on the paper and drew in the smoke but didn't offer it to me again. I felt a little insulted, although I knew I would have refused it.

After a few inhalations, he stubbed the spliff out on the wall and lowered his hand to my waist. He tried to run his other hand up my leg, above my sock. His hands were cold. My skin was stubbly with unshaved hair.

This was not an oversight. It was a tactic. I didn't think I'd let Nicholas touch me with hairy legs. I didn't think I'd get that desperate.

It worked. At least at first. Embarrassed, I moved away from him. I pulled my skirt down, pushed my glasses up my nose. My desire for him when we had talked of Jah or life, the rush that filled my arms and legs and belly, had evaporated.

Nicholas stood up and lit a cigarette. He leaned against the splintered windowsill, smoking. Is he angry at me? I worried. Is he expecting more?

The late hour gave me an unsteady courage. I got up, brushing the dust off my skirt, and stepped close to him. He stubbed out his cigarette and slid his arm around me. I relaxed into him with relief, my ear to his warm chest.

"Come," he said. He flipped on a switch in the hallway. I blinked in the harsh light of a bare bulb, taking in the broken floorboards and the scabs of plaid wallpaper on the dingy walls. I followed Nicholas to the back of the apartment, passing two closed doors. We entered a small, square room with a single window looking out on darkness. There was no furniture, only a paintbrush beside a can of paint in the corner and a broom leaning against the wall. Again, we sat on the floor. I watched his hands approach and cover my breasts. He lay on top of me, heavy. I hugged him, kissing his cheek like I was an actress in a play, powerful and scared at the same time as I acted out things that I had been taught would make my soul burn in hell and repel my future husband.

Nicholas slid one hand under my skirt, his fingers tripping over my knee. Slipping his baggy jeans down, he rubbed his body against mine, a hardness against my underwear.

"No, no," I whispered. I couldn't go this far. I moved my hips away and ran my hand up his neck and into his wiry hair. His hands were back again, picking at the edges of my underwear, his skin touching the shivering skin of my inner thigh, the sensation strange. He pleaded, "Please, princess, lemme just feel, I won' put it inside, please."

It seemed from what he said, from his pursed mouth and narrowed eyes, that he was experiencing some sort of physical anguish that I had caused and that only I could relieve. I didn't want him suffering on my account. I didn't want to be hurting him.

My bra was hitched up, biting into my underarms. He reached for my nipple with his pillowy lips, burying his face in my breast. My skirt tangled around my waist. He pulled my underwear to the side, exposing the patch of hairy skin. His warm body pushed at me.

"Please," I whispered. "Please."

Even in that moment I did not know what I wanted. Please just hold me and comfort me? Please kiss me again, so my face will quiver with electricity? Please stop the tingles of pleasure radiating from my breasts? Please hurry up and get this over with so you'll be satisfied and I can leave? The confusion and desire were impossible to untangle. I lay back and let it roar through me unchecked.

His pushing against my skin became harder. My thigh scraped against the rough floor. "Ow!" I couldn't help crying out. He pulled back as if I had hit him and rolled off me. He lit a cigarette. I jerked my clothing into place, afraid, watching his face. Was he frowning? Was he angry?

"Let's go." Nicholas jerked his chin in the direction of the front door. I followed him out of the apartment in silence. He walked me home in the darkness, wheeling his bike at his side. I kept glancing up at his still face, trying to read its shadowed contours.

"Good night," I said, when we reached my apartment. I looked up at him, hoping for a romantic kiss. But then, suddenly terrified that my landlord or neighbors might be watching from the window, I ran for the door.

That night I lay in bed, reliving Nicholas's touch. I thought about how his muscles jumped in the light, how his chest felt against my breasts. Most of all, I thought about his glorious rush of desire for me, reflected in his glinting eyes.

"Nicholas," I whispered. "Nicholas's girlfriend."

I was flattered to be chosen by him. A man so powerfully exotic. I wanted to make him glad he'd chosen me.

But still, I could not lose my virginity. I put my hand over the front of my underwear as if to protect it.

If I lost my virginity, I couldn't pretend all of this misbehavior was just a phase. I would never be able to marry a yeshiva boy.

In the marriage market of the Yeshivish community, *yichus* was one of the most valuable commodities, and I had it in spades. My father, Rabbi Shaul Kaplan, was a renowned international lecturer who had even been invited to speak at a number of Agudah conventions, a respected voice at the annual meeting of that immensely powerful political lobby. My mother was a descendant of the family of the great Gaon of Vilna. The famous Rabbi Yankev Penchik was my second cousin. But if I wasn't a virgin, none of that would matter. Even if I repented fully, I would be forced to marry a man with divorced parents, or someone obese, or disabled, or who'd become religious later in life, someone whose ignorant throat hacked forth the Hebrew *ch* like phlegm.

chapter seven

ON A SUNDAY I MET NICHOLAS at a bodega underneath the tracks.

"Hey, princess." He kissed me on the cheek. *Princess*. The word fizzled through my body like soda. "Come on," he said.

I followed him down the block and into a dark alley between two apartment buildings.

"You okay?" he asked, leaning his bike against the wall.

I nodded. He ran his hand down my arm and then hugged me, kissing me on the lips. Hip-hop music blasted from a window above us, lending a dangerous rhythm to the movements of our hands as I tried to prove to Nicholas that I was worthy of his interest.

Each night that followed, I waited anxiously in the park, praying for Nicholas. Sometimes he didn't show. But when he did, I looked for the toss of his head or the movement of his chin, his secret summons to slip away from the group of men and follow him to some pool of shadows. I didn't want anyone else in the park to know what I was doing with Nicholas. Even among non-Jews, I feared for my reputation.

I still prayed, tearfully, feeling close to God in the intensity of my emotions, begging for his forgiveness as I violated his commandments. But Nicholas made me feel like I belonged somewhere on earth. Like he cared about me. Like I was special to him.

My mother called occasionally. Our conversations were terse. I wanted her to tell me she missed me. I wanted her to say that she worried about everything that had happened with me over the past few years, and to ask if we could talk about it. I wanted her to mention that she was looking into someone for me, a good learner, a smart boy. But she never said anything strong enough to pull me away from Nicholas.

My parents were spending the summer in Lakewood, New Jersey—the heart of the Yeshivish world, just two hours out of Brooklyn. The next time I spoke to my mother, I asked her if I could visit for Shabbos.

She was quiet for a moment. "Well," she finally said, "it's Mordy's birthday on Shabbos. Okay. You can come if you'd like."

Four and a half years younger than me, Mordy was the seventh child out of eleven. A clever, bright-eyed kid, he always had his face buried in a book. I was shocked to hear that he was already turning twelve. It was hard to accept that life was going on without me. He probably barely remembers me, I realized, hanging up the phone. I was sure they didn't talk about me.

In my family, birthdays were celebrated with a homemade cake, but I decided to get Mordy a gift. A gift might make him feel special in the way that I always wanted to feel special. And maybe it would keep him from forgetting me.

On Thursday evening, I found a toy store on Sixteenth Avenue. I browsed the bright mountains of board games and LEGO sets. Mordy was turning twelve, the last birthday before his Bar Mitzvah. He would be sent away to yeshiva in a year. A twelve-year-old boy should already be serious about his studies. I left the toy store and passed a Judaica shop. I could get him a holy book, I thought, but he probably had plenty of those already. I'll buy him a shirt, I decided, stepping into a men's clothing store. He was probably wearing hand-me-downs from Elisha. I imagined that he might be nervous about going away to yeshiva, where all the kids from New York would have crisp shirts, and his would be grubby and gray at the collar.

"I'll take a pair of cuff links too," I told the Hasid behind the counter. If I skipped lunch a couple times, I could afford the smallest pair of ribbed golden squares nestled in the velvet display case. Mordy would look sharp when he showed up to yeshiva. He would look like a cool kid. I stood on my tiptoes, peering over the counter as the man wrapped my selections in white tissue paper, securing the package with a bubble of tape.

"For a *chusson?*" he asked. His English rumbled with a Yiddish accent.

I giggled nervously. "No, my brother." I had no fiancé.

I was not sure if my little brothers would remember me, but they sidled up to me shyly when I came through the door, grins on their faces. "Oh my gosh, you've all gotten so big!" I cried, hugging them close. They laughed and squirmed away. I said hello to my mother, accepting her awkward hug.

"I have something for you," I called to Mordy, kicking off my shoes and throwing my bags down in the bedroom I was going to share with my fifteen-year-old sister, Deena.

"What is it?" he asked, tossing his book aside and running after me. Boorie Tzvi and Yanky trailed behind him. I unzipped my book bag and pulled the neat package from under my balled-up Shabbos clothes. The boys hovered at my elbows, eyes wide.

"Happy birthday." I handed over the gift.

"Thanks." Mordy beamed. He ripped open the paper.

"Do you like it?" I asked.

He nodded shyly. "Thanks, I'm gonna go get ready for Shabbos!"

I laughed as he ran off. There were still three hours before Shabbos began.

"What did you get us?" Boorie Tzvi asked, sliding his yarmulke to the back of his head and poking at my bag.

"Yeah, what about uth?" Yanky echoed, his lisp cutting off his words.

"I'm sorry," I said. "I'll get you something when it's your birthday, if I'm here. Come, I'll read you a book instead."

Boorie Tzvi was too miffed to follow me to the couch, but Yanky brought over a book and nestled his scrawny little body into my side.

At the Shabbos meal, my father chose Mordy and Yanky to sit on either side of him, Mordy in the place that used to be mine. He avoided my eyes and didn't direct any questions at me. I stayed silent as my siblings jumped at his attention. I ate two bowls of soup and two chicken thighs at each meal that weekend and asked for a third piece of pineapple kugel, as if it could stave off the hunger I knew was waiting for me back in Brooklyn.

On Shabbos afternoon, the next day, I found my mother sitting in the kitchen. She was wearing a simple black Shabbos robe and a black snood edged in rhinestones. Without the distraction of a styled wig, the creases under her eyes and around her lips seemed deeper. The eye shadow and lipstick she had applied heavily before Shabbos had faded by now, leaving her features bare.

When I was young, my mother had worn long wavy wigs and jewel-toned sweaters and a paisley brown Shabbos robe shot through with gold threads. But the rules of modesty seemed to get stricter every year, and Yeshivish women were no longer allowed to dress so flamboyantly.

"Can I ask you something?" I said, approaching her.

She looked up from her magazine, a Yeshivish women's monthly.

"What is it?"

"I wanted to talk to you about something."

"The baby might wake in a moment," she said, glancing down the hallway toward the bedroom. "But sit down. We can talk until then."

"You know," I said, taking a deep breath, "I have new friends now. I've met some people, in the park near my apartment." I pushed my glasses up my nose, folded my arms, watched my mother's eyes harden and one arched eyebrow lift.

"I like them," I said. "They're my friends." *I'm lonely* was what I meant. *I miss you. I feel abandoned.*

My mother wrinkled her nose but said nothing.

"They look out for me," I said, pushing further. "They're not Jewish, but they really like me."

I both feared and hoped that my mother would yell at me for having non-Jewish friends, but instead she looked at me long and hard and then turned back to the magazine.

"You like them because you're so much better than them. They are trash, Leah. Trash." She bit off that final word, her eyes on the page.

But I couldn't walk away. I needed her to rescue me from my rebellion. I hadn't planned to hint at the whole truth, but I couldn't help myself.

"I mean—" I cleared my throat, afraid to form the words. "If—if, you know, if something would happen, with a man, you know, if I—slept with one, would you sit shivah for me, would you treat me like I was dead?"

My mother looked up at me with a hasty glance, as if to judge how seriously to consider my words, then nodded a quick yes. She pursed her lips and turned back to her magazine. The conversation was over.

Disappointed by my inability to get her attention, I trudged back to my bedroom. How could my mother be so uninvested in my life, I wondered. Had she ever loved me at all?

At that time, I did not know nothing about sex. By the age of seventeen, I had amassed a fair amount of knowledge about that thing which could not be named:

1. In seventh grade, I learned through the grapevine that babies were made by mothers and fathers getting naked and rubbing their bodies together. I was quite certain that religious people did not have to undertake such a shameful and sinful activity. Looking over the evidence—what I knew about modesty, babies, and this unnameable thing—I concluded that religious people got pregnant by kissing. God would have to give us that dispensation.
2. A few years before seventh grade, I myself had gotten naked and rubbed my body up against the body of another little girl.
3. I did not make the connection between what I had done and how babies were made. Shame can be fantastic at inducing amnesia. One does not really forget, but the humiliation of remembering is so great, one can maintain a careful ignorance of the past, handicapping one's brain from reaching logical conclusions.
4. In eighth grade, Tiffany Lewis, the most popular girl in our class, had once bestowed upon me the honor of letting me join her on the walk home from school. Like many of my classmates in Pittsburgh, the Lewis family was barely Orthodox. "I asked my older sister what you did with it," Tiffany had said to me. "That's what I didn't understand—you know what I'm talking about, right?" I nodded wildly. Even then I was good at pretending I knew more than I did. "My sister told me you could spit or swallow," she said. I understood enough

to know that this had something to do with sex, something to do with a man's penis and a woman's mouth. But it remained an isolated factoid without context until five years later, three minutes after the first time I wrapped my own lips around a penis; at that moment it came back to me, and I understood, as I gagged, that Tiffany had been giving me a rare and useful tip for a life that I was otherwise ill prepared for.

5. A woman's vagina was a lump of hairy skin with a seam across it.

6. In Bais Esther, in Israel, I got ahold of some tampons for the first time. Crouched over the dormitory toilet, I held the black-and-white drawing the manufacturers had provided in one hand as I poked a cardboard tube at my vagina with the other. From this drawing I learned that beyond the seam, through the meaty innards that seemed solid enough, one could find a tunnel of sorts, which probably led to the stomach.

7. At some point along the way, I learned about sperm, the thing that came from a man's penis at the end of sex and made a baby in a woman's stomach.

8. When I was sixteen, a married religious woman had confided in me that while she'd learned the facts of life, like every Yeshivish girl, in special "bride classes" before her wedding, she had been taken unawares by her new husband's interest in her breasts, which she, like I, had assumed would become the exclusive property of her nursing babies. I had plenty of experience with men talking to my breasts, but, apparently, there was more than staring. The woman didn't go into specifics, but it was another placeholder of knowledge. Daniel and Nicholas had already begun to demonstrate how this worked, and I would soon learn that it was a common opening move in the awkward dance of one body entering another.

A few days after I got back from Lakewood, Nicholas told me to meet him in Manhattan at a club called Starlight. His brother worked there, he said. I washed and braided my hair and dressed in my gray pleated skirt, white blouse, and Shabbos heels. Running up the steps to the train station that ran over McDonald Avenue, I found a token in the creases of my purse, pushed through the turnstile, and dashed up to the platform suspended in a black forest of rooftops. The F train came roaring down the track, shaking to a stop before me.

At Forty-second Street, I slipped through the clumps of tourists that jammed the sidewalk, making my way north. Buses, cars, and taxis fought for space on the road, filling the air with the sooty smell of exhaust. Tall buildings draped with giant signs advertising drinks and television shows crowded out the sky. The short blocks went by quickly as I wove my way around the dawdling visitors and the brash natives, taking in the storefronts piled high with colorful merchandise, wondering what lives were lived in the thousands of windows that rose above my head. Before I knew it, I was at the club, on Fifty-fourth Street. Lines of people waited in front of silver-framed smoky glass doors. I spotted Nicholas leaning against the next building over, his hair covered with a knit cap, hands jammed in his pockets. I felt dangerous and glamorous approaching him, claiming him.

"Hey!"

"Hey, princess." He kissed my cheek. I closed my eyes, savoring the soft give of his lips on my skin.

He led me around the crowd of men and women waiting outside the club, to a side door. Inside, in the narrow hallways, guitar twangs and drum crashes pummeled the air. I followed Nicholas down into the unfinished basement, where the music faded to a muffled thumping. We entered a big, dimly lit room. The blue light of a small television at the back flickered over an odd array of furniture. We settled on a couch. I ran an anxious hand over the cushion, which left a gritty layer of grime on my fingers. I moved forward, closer to the edge, hoping not to dirty my skirt. My eyes were drawn to the television, a forbidden appliance. I kept ripping my eyes from the screen, trying to escape its magnetic grasp.

Nicholas slouched beside me, legs spread wide, eyes glinting toward the TV. He slid his hand around my waist. His smell of bitter sweat and pungent marijuana made my heart beat fast. On the television screen, a policeman ran through trees and bushes, shouting:

"Get down! Put your weapon down now!"

Without looking at me, Nicholas ran his other hand over my thighs. He lifted my skirt. He turned and leaned on top of me, clutching at my breasts. I held on to his back. We were both breathing hard. I watched his bright eyes as he fumbled at his waist. His hand skimmed the skin of my hips. He pulled my underwear to the side at the crotch, combing for my insides. He was focused, intense. My excitement was mixed with fear.

"No," I whispered. "Sweetheart, I don't want—" His hard penis brushed against my thigh. He opened my dry skin.

"No, Nicholas." It couldn't go this far. I couldn't let this happen.

But if it did. If he did. That would be how they always said it would go. That would be a man reacting to the power of my body the way I had been taught. And God wouldn't hold me responsible if I'd said no, would he?

"No, please—" But now I meant it, as he pushed at me, as my flirtation with danger was overcome by his very real insistence. "It hurts—please—stop—"

His full mouth fell over mine. I squeezed my eyes shut and kissed him desperately, as if he could swallow me whole, suck me out of the moment.

He pushed into me, splitting my tight flesh with a wide blunt knife.

He sawed away at me, falling over my shoulder. My hands fell against the couch, still under his moving body. After a few long moments, he stopped and pulled back. Blinking back tears, I watched him withdraw to the corner of the couch.

Women screamed on the television.

My insides burned.

Was that—sex? I couldn't feel any blood, only a dry agony. I looked over at Nicholas, his face obscured in the darkness. I became afraid that I had upset him. I couldn't lose him. No matter what, I couldn't lose this man. Not after what had just happened, whatever it was.

"Are . . . are you okay?" I whispered. I scanned his face, terrified that I had disappointed him. That he didn't care for me anymore.

He wouldn't meet my eyes.

I couldn't invite him back into my body; my insides were throbbing with pain. But I was desperate. I leaned into Nicholas's lap, reached into his pants, and took his long, limp penis in my hand. I put the end of it in my mouth, unsure of how my lips and tongue and teeth and gums were supposed to interact with his body. Nicholas grabbed my head and pushed it down onto his suddenly erect penis, which was leaping with life, ramming my throat. Tears burned in my eyes as I gagged. After a few minutes, he ejected a slimy mess on my tongue. I coughed, spitting it out onto the floor. I wiped my lips on my sleeve and fixed my glasses. Nicholas put a hand on my shoulder and I curled up next to him, pushing back tears, pleased that I'd been able to produce such a powerful thing in him. Pleased that I hadn't lost him.

"Meet me here tomorrow at six?" Nicholas asked when he walked me to the train later that night. I nodded. He kissed me lightly on the cheek, and we said good-bye.

As I rode back to Brooklyn, I stared out the window, into the dark tunnels of the subway, replaying the touch of Nicholas's skin on mine, picturing his sparkling eyes, the hunger for me on his face and in his body. I kept my legs crossed, applying pressure to the spot where the burn still emanated as the echoes of the evening flashed across my weary mind. That was sex, a voice in my head tried to tell me. There may not have been any blood, but that was definitely the thing called sex. My inner voice seemed to come from somewhere outside of me, looking down on my tingling body.

When I got home, I stripped to my underwear and climbed into bed, burying my nose in my elbow to block the stink of rotting banana peels that poured out of the garbage can.

In the middle of the night, I woke with a shudder from a nightmare of giant fingers ripping my limbs to pieces, like a chicken pulled apart in my mother's hands. The apartment was still. I hugged my pillow and whispered the psalms I knew by heart to keep the dark at bay.

"Hey, princess." The next evening, a pair of arms enveloped me from behind, pulling me into a hug. I stumbled backward into Nicholas's chest, breathing in his smell of soap, marijuana, and stale cigarettes.

We left the bustle of Fifty-fourth Street, entering the dark, silent club. I followed him down the stairs and into a smaller room in the basement that contained only a metal bench peppered with rust and shelves of broken cardboard boxes along the walls. The air reeked of ammonia.

"You okay?" Nicholas asked, closing the door behind us.

I nodded, releasing my hand from my skirt, which I had been clutching nervously. *What am I doing here?* I wondered. *Leah—this* shvartze—*what are you doing with him?*

Nicholas took a step toward me. "Take it off." He pointed his chin at my body, my clothes.

"What's your last name?" I asked, meekly scraping the words out of my throat.

"Whachu askin'?" Nicholas folded his arms.

"Your last name. What's your last name? I don't even know

it." I forced myself to be strong, although I feared he would turn and leave angrily.

He laughed. "Wright. Nicholas Jason Wright. That okay with you?"

I nodded.

"Then take it off."

He watched with his arms folded as I flailed out of my shirt and skirt and removed my underwear and bra. He had never seen me without my clothes. No man ever had. My breasts, my stomach, my thighs—they seemed to take up too much space, chunks of unwieldy fat affixed to a trembling core. I backed up and sat on the bench, the metal cold on my bare behind. Nicholas came to me and gently lay me down, covering my body with his. The lightness of his touch filled my heart. I relaxed.

"Nicholas," I whispered, squeezing a hand between my breasts and his T-shirt.

"What's that?" he said softly and bent his head to kiss my nipple, brushing my mouth with his wiry hair. My skin vibrated with pleasure.

"No, wait, Nicholas." I hesitated until he looked up at me.

"Do you love me, Nicholas?" My eyes welled with tears.

"Shit, girl. Don't cry. Yes, I love you. I love you, princess."

Princess. I smiled and sniffed. He stretched his neck up and kissed my lips.

"All good?" he asked.

"All good," I whispered.

He pulled his jeans and boxers down. I opened my thighs and closed my eyes. My body went rigid as his body bore into it, slicing me up, sanding me down.

He moaned as he moved. I opened my eyes. His glittering eyes and his open mouth looked like love.

"Leah, Leah. I'm gonna come!"

He pulled out of me, leaving air to kiss my stinging insides as he spewed a soupy puddle onto the floor. "Ahhh," he said with a shudder, stepping back. He grabbed a rag off a shelf and wiped his penis clean.

I struggled back into my clothes. He turned on a record player that was on the floor.

"Don' worry 'bout a thing. 'Cause every little thing's gonna be all right." The singer's cool voice filled the room. Nicholas flashed his big teeth at me and ran his hand down my arm.

"C'mon," he said. He led me to the room we had been in the night before and turned on a lamp. He switched on the television and sat on the couch. I sat beside him, slipping off my shoes, tucking my leg beneath me, secretly pressing my heel into my crotch to press down the pain.

"I'm gonna call in some chicken—you want some, princess?"

I shook my head. "Kosher, remember?" I wasn't hungry anyhow.

In the weeks that followed, the terrifying comprehension that I had destroyed my future caught me in waves. Ironically, my respite was with Nicholas. Although the act of sex was only mildly pleasant at most, I felt euphoric counting the hours until we could be together in the basement of Starlight. I polished my wanting with my imagination, savoring the image of him reaching for me, desire reflected in his eyes. All day long I thought about his warm breath on my eager face, his heart thumping against my chest, skin to skin, toe to toe, eye to eye, knowing that I was the only thing he saw in those moments, knowing I was the only person in his world.

chapter eight

I HAD JUST STEPPED OUT THE DOOR on the morning of Rosh Hashanah Eve, rushing to Manhattan for a half day of work, when I heard the phone ring. I ran back inside. Nicholas hadn't called or picked up his phone in five days. I had left him seven messages, worried. He had always been slow to return my calls, and he rarely answered his phone, but he had never been silent for this long. I had started listening to the news on the radio, afraid that the police might have found the marijuana I had discovered he stored in the roots of his dreadlocks, for his own frequent consumption and to sell to others. Smiling with relief, I grabbed the phone.

"Leah?"

"Oh." It was my mother.

"You okay? Everything is okay?"

"Yes."

"I'm calling to ask for forgiveness. You should know that everything I do, I do for your best, and I always ask a rabbi if I have any questions. But nonetheless, if I did anything that also hurt your feelings in some way, I hope you'll forgive me. HaShem should forgive all of us. We should all have a happy, healthy year."

"Okay," I whispered.

"Have a good Yom Tov. I've got to go, good-bye."

I slammed the phone down and struggled to take in a breath

as frustration and despair and fury rose higher and higher in my body, like a typhoon in a glass bottle.

It was the tradition to ask for forgiveness in the High Holiday season, in hope that others relinquishing their grudges would sway a stern God to pardon our sins. Would there, I fumed, be such easy forgiveness for me? *If I did anything that also hurt your feelings in some way?* Is she fucking kidding or is she just completely oblivious? Exasperated, I shook my head.

When I got home from work later that day, I called Nicholas again, praying for him to finally answer his phone.

"Nicholas," I yelped when he picked up.

"What up?"

"I was worried about you. You didn't call. I left messages."

"Yeah. Coffee had my phone."

"It's a holiday, a Jewish holiday tonight, for two days. I can't call you—I just wanted to let you know."

"Okay."

"Okay, so I'll call you when it's done, okay? On Thursday night."

"Okay."

"I love you so much, Nicholas."

"Me, too."

Me too. That didn't sound very convincing.

I needed to do something. I couldn't lose Nicholas. I had given him my virginity. He had to be my everything. He had no choice. I put the phone down and slowly made my way to the refrigerator to rustle up some dinner.

The year before I'd left Pittsburgh for Manchester, my breasts had swollen, shrinking my bras to tiny triangles over my nipples. I had skipped a few meals, hoping losing weight would reduce them, but it seemed to have no effect. Finally I had waited until my mother was alone in the kitchen, flipping through a religious magazine, eating a peanut butter rice cake iced with banana slices.

"Ma," I had said.

"What is it?"

"I need a——" I didn't know how to say it. The word "bra" wouldn't come out. It was too grossly immodest.

My mother slid her fingers under her snood to tuck away a wisp of exposed hair.

"What is it?"

"Can I have some money to go to Mrs. Schultz?" I asked, my cheeks burning with embarrassment. Mrs. Schultz sold bras in her basement. "I—I need new underwear."

"Oh." My mother nodded. "Yes. Of course. Take forty dollars from my purse. Remember to bring back the change."

Mrs. Schultz sold me two ivory bras with wire in the seams and wide straps that dug hot-pink tracks into my shoulders. She promised me that they minimized my chest by two sizes, but I was not convinced.

Now those bras were peeling and gray at the edges. My underwear, slack-waisted, hand-me-downs from my older sisters, were in worse condition.

Maybe that's the problem, I thought as I lay in bed after whispering the Shema. Maybe I'm wearing the wrong underwear. I remembered that one night Star, a Puerto Rican girl from the park, had bent over to tie her shoelaces, revealing an electric-pink string tight around her waist. And most of the time, Star's lacy bra straps were clearly visible beside the straps of her tank tops. Maybe I needed underwear like Star's. Maybe then Nicholas would be into me again.

A few days later, after work ended, I walked down Broadway, shivering in the cool autumn breeze. The evening was gray with the approaching twilight, and the air filled with the sweet aroma of honey-roasted nuts hawked from sidewalk stalls. I moved through the crowds, enjoying the steady rhythm of my heels on the pavement, passing block after block before I finally paused in front of a shop featuring headless mannequins clad in colorful lingerie. I took a quick shallow breath and pushed the door open, setting off a clanging bell.

The walls of the shop were crammed with bright bits of provocative lace and ribbons. I had never been to a store like this. Embarrassed, I turned to leave.

"Can I help you?" asked an older black woman, stepping in front of me. "Are you looking for something?"

"Um, well, I'm looking for, for—underwear."

"Panties?" the woman asked.

The word humiliated me. For all of my sexual behavior, there were remnants of modesty that I had not yet shaken off. The saleswoman took my silence as a yes and ushered me over to a far wall.

"Now, were you looking for something in particular?"

"Um, underwear," I repeated, humiliated.

"This is the underwear section, dear. Are you looking for bras? For panties? We have boy-cut underwear here, and thongs here—" The woman lifted a garment between her long orange nails. It looked like the thing Star had worn, a triangle of cloth dangling from a string. The underwear on display embarrassed me too much for me to make my choice in front of the saleswoman.

"Thank you," I said, and pushed into a rack of more traditional pairs of panties, inspecting the tags. Once the woman was out of sight, I grabbed a thong and scrunched it into a small ball, so as not to be noticed by the other shoppers. I made my way quickly to the cashier and passed it over the counter, along with a handful of quarters. I didn't have enough money for a new bra as well. I hoped this exotic garment would be enough to do the trick.

When I got home, I took the underwear out of the shopping

bag, pulling the stretchy fabric in my hands. It looked like an imbalanced hourglass, the tag dangling from the smaller end. That made no sense. How could the small triangle be meant to cover my bottom? It must be a mistake, I decided, but I snipped off the tag with a pair of scissors so there would be no evidence of my confusion. I pulled the garment on, small piece in front, larger piece behind. The fabric dug into my butt, filling me with an urge to relieve myself of its wedgie-like pressure, but when I looked in the mirror, I loved its crazy goyishness. I turned on the balls of my feet, admiring the garment stretched over my plump behind. It felt glamorously wicked.

I went down to the bodega by the park. Coffee and two other guys stood outside, leaning against the wall. They reached out to kiss my cheek hello. I tensed at this welcome. Kissing Nicholas was one thing. Kissing these men felt like a waste of a sin.

"Is Nicholas here?" I asked.

"Nah," Coffee said. "I ain't seen him."

I walked down the block, peering into the dark spaces between the apartment buildings where we often made out. A cat sauntered out of the darkness and around my legs, but otherwise the street was still.

Frustrated and disappointed, itching to pull the thong off, I went home. If only Nicholas could see me now, I thought. I imagined his eyes lighting up the way they used to, at the sight of my new underwear. I imagined him looking at me again like a lion eyeing a slab of bloody meat. Wanting me that much. Never wanting to let me go.

When I got home, I dialed Nicholas's cell phone. It rang and rang.

"Nicholas, hey, Nicholas, it's me. I miss you. Call me back, okay? I—I really miss you. Can you call me, please?"

I had been groomed to handle men—God, my father, my future husband—with relentless worship. I carried that lesson from my childhood into my relationship with Nicholas and beyond, like a butterfly dragging its cocoon.

"What up?" Nicholas said when we finally saw each other. He ran his hand over my butt, his usual greeting. He stopped. He looked at me, slid his hand into the waistband of my denim skirt, and ran his cold fingers over my bare behind.

"Damn," he said. "No more granny panties, huh?"

Humiliated, I cringed. I had been wearing the wrong kind of underwear all along. Perhaps now, with my new thong, we would go back to how we used to be.

But the thong was not enough to save our relationship. Nicholas's phone continued to ring and ring. Voice-mail messages went unreturned. One evening, I came home from work and sat down to a dinner of an apple and a handful of cookies. Dialing his number for the third time, my fingers dancing over the buttons in that familiar pattern, it surprised me to suddenly hear the interruption of his voice.

"I've been trying to get through to you for weeks and weeks. What's wrong? Where are you?" I asked.

"Starlight."

"Really? I just got back from the city. I wish I knew. I really want to see you. Do you want to see me?"

"Yep."

"Do you want me to come over?"

"Yeah."

"But it's so late already. Okay. I'll come over—I'll get there in about an hour. You'll be there still?"

"Uh-huh."

"All right, I'll see you soon. I love you."

"Okay."

• • •

Nicholas sat low on the big couch. He picked up a porn magazine lying on a cushion. I perched on the leather armchair in the corner. He dug a joint out of his pocket and lit it, sucking hard on the paper.

"Hey, look at this." He pointed to a picture of a naked pregnant woman in the magazine. I had seen the porn magazines and lewd posters scattered around the basement of Starlight before. I always averted my eyes. This picture bothered me even more than the others. The idea that a mother, and a pregnant one at that, would pose so crudely made my stomach turn. A pregnant woman was sacred. She was fulfilling her destiny. It sickened me that a woman in that condition would display herself naked for men.

"I really don't want to see." Why are you so interested in her, I thought. She's a picture. I'm here. I'm sitting right here, right in front of you. What the fuck is so deformed about me that you aren't interested?

"C'mon, look!"

"I'm not interested!"

He shrugged and kept reading, the rise and fall of his breath filling the silence. I stared at him, willing him to look up, willing him to speak to me, but his eyes were glued to the page. I did not know how to get through to him. I did not know how to seduce him. I thought my body itself was my most potent tool, but it seemed that its mere availability was not enough. It seemed that I was not enough.

I left the room, my chest tight, and went inside the broom closet. Pulled the string for the light. Closed the door. Everything thrown at this man for nothing, I thought. It hurts. It hurts. I couldn't catch my breath. A nail sat on the wooden shelf. Long and pointy and orange with rust. I rolled it in my fingers, wiped the dust on the bottom of my shirt. I felt like a balloon of pain, swollen to almost bursting. Nicholas. Nicholas. Why won't you look at me? I tested the edge of the nail on the pad of my finger. I should hurt myself, I thought. I should push the nail right through my fucking finger. I listened for noise in the hallway. Nobody was calling after me. It was suddenly clear. Nicholas was a bum. A drug dealer. An uneducated loser. Someone who wore his pants low on his butt, looked at porn, drank forties, and smoked marijuana and cigarettes all day long. A typical goy. He didn't know how to love me. I had wasted my love. I had wasted my virginity. The thought of my stupidity pulled my lips back in a grimace. I yanked back my skirt and drew the nail across my leg. It left a white trail. *I can't breathe. I can't breathe.* Nicholas. Nicholas! Now pink streaks. Then, at last, blood. The bright red drops surprised me. Triumphant, I went back to the room, holding the skirt away from my leg. I didn't want to lose my proof.

"Look what I did," I said to Nicholas. "You don't understand when I tell you I miss you or that I'm upset, so I'm showing you how I feel."

He looked at my leg, then at my face. He was high. His eyelids drooped; his arms hung loose on the couch.

"Whachu do that wit'?" he asked.

"A nail." I was defiant. Proud. Poised for a fight. For a hug. For a talking to. Ready to scream back. Ready to tussle. Ready to collapse, crying, in his arms.

Nicholas shook his head and laughed.

"You loco. You loco, girl." His eyes drifted back to his magazine. I stood there, skirt gathered in my fist, leg bleeding. I stood there and stared at him. He turned the page of his magazine. He kept his eyes on the naked women on the pages in front of him.

My stomach ached as I made my way home. I was done with Nicholas. It was over. My sadness solidified into metal shards that poked at my insides.

The pain in my belly lingered in the days that followed, sometimes doubling me over. At work I sat scrunched down in my chair.

"Is something the matter, hon?" Lakisha asked.

"I have a stomachache. I dunno. It's been hurting for a while."

"Did you take Advil?"

"No. I think I'm just lactose intolerant or something. I'm gonna try and stop drinking milk."

I'd thought I had it all figured out. I'd thought I knew the reason for everything.

Lakisha passed me a bottle of ibuprofen. I took two pills, but the pain did not subside.

Ocean Parkway was a solid mass of frozen cars. The trees that lined the avenue danced and billowed in the wind, while the late-afternoon traffic inched and stalled, stuttering across the short blocks.

"Please, can you drive a little bit faster?" I begged the car service driver.

"Faster? Faster?" He waved his puffy hand at the cars in front of him. The red lights seemed to slam down whenever a space opened on the road. "No faster, miss."

I buried my face in the seat.

"Please, please, please," I whimpered, pressing my knees into my breasts, trying to relieve the pain in my stomach, which had grown so large it felt like an animal was ripping its claws through my abdomen.

In the crowded emergency room, I pushed through the people clustered at the window to sign my name. As I waited to be called, I breathed heavily to hold back the tears.

"Leah Kaplan?" I sprang forward. "How old are you?" the nurse asked.

"Seventeen," I gasped.

The nurse clucked, shaking her head, braids swinging over her shoulders. "Seventeen? You need to go down to pediatrics."

I hobbled down the hall, pressing my fists into my stomach, sucking air through my nostrils. The waiting room was filled with mothers and fathers holding their children close to their chests. The air was thick with love. No. I couldn't wait here.

I caught the attention of a male nurse.

"Please," I sobbed. "I'm in pain, can you help me?"

The nurse ushered me inside. He took down my information and found me a bed to wait on before he was called away. I crouched over the mattress, crying.

A lady standing with a child by the next bed tapped me on the shoulder. "Wha's wrong wit' yo baby?"

My baby? What baby? I screamed, grinding my face into the mattress. The woman backed away, calling out apologies. I was seventeen years old, without a husband or baby in sight, just an agonizing stomachache and a broken heart.

"Please," I sobbed when the nurse passed my bed again. "Please can I have something to stop the pain?"

He shrugged his shoulders sympathetically. "I'm sorry, but we can't give you anything yet. We can't admit you."

"Why not?" I gasped, trying to force my voice over the clenching agony that was working its way across my abdomen.

"We need parental permission because you're a minor. We called your mom in Pennsylvania, but she won't let us admit you. But—you know what—I'll have one of the doctors call her now, explain." The nurse patted my foot and hurried away.

I could not understand what my mother might be thinking to deny me relief, to deny me emergency medical care. I didn't know what the nurse had told her. I wondered if she thought I was in the hospital because of something sinful I had done. If she thought I was choking on a cheeseburger or cradling an arm broken by a non-Jewish friend. If she was thinking, *Good, let her suffer.*

"At the end of the day, family is always family," my mother had often told me when I complained about my sisters' constant teasing. No, I thought, as the room around me shimmered. I am no longer family. I am nothing. I am trash.

Somehow, the nurse got my mother to agree to have me admitted. He stabbed my arms with his needle as he tried to find one of my small veins. When the needle was set and the IV fixed, the drugs rushed in. I was shocked by a euphoric rush of air as I breathed my first full breath in weeks, no pain waiting to suck it away. I sank into the bed, exhausted with relief.

"It's an ovarian cyst," the doctor told me, after I'd drunk thirty-two ounces of water and had undergone a sonogram. "It's painfully twisted. It's not an irregular occurrence. We'll operate later today and remove the cyst. That will eliminate your pain."

I called work to explain that I was sick. I couldn't bring myself to talk of my ovaries, so I said I had a stomach virus. I wasn't sure how my job's health insurance was processed, but I hoped it wouldn't betray my lie to my boss.

I was grateful that I had insurance, but I knew it might not cover all of the medical bills I was about to incur, and I was still just scraping by. I was too numb to fear for my body, but the state of my finances scared me. I dialed my parents' number.

"Ma?"

"Yes?"

"It's Leah."

"Yes?" Her abruptness dried up any small talk I might have used to cushion what I wanted to say. I sat hunched over in the hospital bed, the receiver pressed to my ear, feeling the warm recycled air on my exposed back, playing with the plastic bracelet on my wrist, looking for the right words, afraid my mother would end the call if I didn't spit something out quickly.

"So, you know I'm in the hospital," I finally said. "I have to have a procedure done, and I don't know if my insurance will cover it, and I'm just a little nervous. If I need help, can you help me with the bills?"

"No," she said. "You're on your own."

My jaw dropped at the curtness of her response. "What the hell?" I cried, my nervous calm punctured. "Don't you even want to know what's wrong with me? Don't you want to know how I feel?"

"Excuse me?" My mother reacted to my taboo curse word. "What did you just say?"

"I don't understand why you treat me like garbage," I sobbed. "It's disgusting. You have no idea how to be a normal mother. You're just—"

But I was attacking a dead line. She had already hung up.

Emerging from the anesthesia after the surgery, I saw a small circle of light appear above me. I hovered in a state of nothingness. Sink into the darkness, I thought. It beckoned like a warm bed on a lazy morning. Why fight? What's waiting for you up there?

You have to fight, I thought. You have to keep fighting. But the blackness was like syrup, pulling me down.

Still, some internal force would not let me go. With great effort, I lifted up into consciousness, out of the anesthesia, blinking awake in a quiet hospital room. I lay limp, my eyes half-open, until a group of doctors came by. They lifted my gown and examined the bandages on my stomach.

"Do you have any questions?" one of the doctors asked as I modestly rearranged the hospital gown. He folded his arms across his chest.

My throat was scratchy. I couldn't put words to my fears. I was afraid to say the wrong thing in front of these dignified men. The doctors nodded, turned to leave.

"Can you tell me what you did in the surgery?" I blurted out.

The main doctor stopped. He glanced at the man to his left. He looked down at his shoes.

"Well," he said, "we'll talk about it later." The group quickly shuffled out.

I berated myself for asking what was apparently a demanding question. I stayed quiet when the nurses came in to check on the IV and my blood pressure. The surgeon, a short Pakistani man with a shiny pompadour, finally came by to check on me the next day.

"Well, hello there, Ms. Kaplan. You're feeling all right now?"

I nodded.

"You should be all set to be released this afternoon. And the surgery. I was hearing you wanted me to review what occurred during the surgery?"

"Yes, please," I said.

"We made three small incisions in your abdomen," he said. "In fact, the twisted cyst was minuscule and not in a position that would cause pain."

"I—I don't understand. Then what was wrong with the cyst?"

The doctor pursed his lips.

"The problem was not a cyst," he said rapidly. "It was pelvic inflammatory disease. The immediate infection should respond well to the antibiotics we've been giving you. Here, I have a brochure."

"Pelvic Inflammatory Disease" was typed on the cover, above a photograph of a woman with a smooth blonde bob, smiling broadly, chin resting in her hand. Her expression seemed to imply that pelvic inflammatory disease was about as delightful as a basketful of kittens. I read, "PID occurs when bacteria from the vagina or cervix enter the uterus, fallopian tubes, ovaries, or pelvis. The most common way to develop PID is by having unprotected sex with someone who has a sexually transmitted infection. PID is the leading cause of infertility. One episode of the disease can cause infertility in 13% of women."

A sexually transmitted infection. I knew about those. Like

AIDS. I had seen an advertisement once on the subway that I could never erase from my memory: a man, emaciated like a Holocaust survivor, his cheeks hollow, his hands too large.

I thought about all the times I had been with Nicholas over the summer and early fall. How many "episodes" of the disease had I contracted? What did those percentages add up to, in terms of my fertility? One hundred percent, probably. Divine punishment was rarely half-assed. I had been waiting for the other shoe to drop all along. And now it had. The inevitable mold that permeated a sinful life had begun to stake its claim.

I would have hoped for a broken bone. A robbery. A twenty-pound weight gain. To lose my fertility was not a mild slap on the behind. It was a complete eclipse of my future self.

I knew only one Yeshivish woman without children. My cousin Malka from Philadelphia. When we saw Malka at weddings, the other married cousins would shake their heads and whisper, eyeing her stomach. Malka's husband was frequently honored with the task of carrying baby boys into their circumcision, but his wife never got pregnant. Had she been to holy rabbis for blessings? everyone wondered. Had she eaten the tip of an *esrog*, the citron used during the holiday of Sukkus that some believed contained mystical power? Malka's infertility was like a large mole on the end of her nose. It was impossible to look at her without seeing her flaw. Without a child clinging to her skirt and another on her hip, Malka's impeccably elegant wig, gentle nature, and fantastic apple crumble kugel didn't matter at all.

I closed my eyes, my body heavy on the thin mattress, the brochure gripped in my hand. My breath was sharp and quick through my nostrils. My heart knocked hard in my chest. Beyond the open door, the day moved ahead. Nurses laughed and a male voice called for a woman named Erma.

chapter nine

INTRODUCTION TO PSYCHOLOGY WAS IN James Hall. But I couldn't match up the large brick buildings with the squares on my map. I could feel the sweat on my back as I strode up and down the walk, trying to find the names on the buildings. I also needed to pee. Desperately.

Why'd you think you could do this? I asked myself. *Can't even decipher a fucking map. College student? Who are you kidding?*

When I'd been released from the hospital, I'd felt infused with a rush of energy. It was apparent that I would not sail directly into the life of an ordinary Yeshivish girl. That was an unavoidable fact. If I couldn't have children, no normal Yeshivish boy would ever want me. It was time, I realized, to pursue the dream sparked by that conversation with Jacob and Naftali so long ago. A Yeshivish girl who could fall for a Rastafarian drug dealer should be bold enough to go to college.

I had passed Brooklyn College many times on my walks through the borough, peering through the black spiked fence at the men and women who sauntered along the paths. They seemed to radiate privilege, so comfortable in their roles as students, taking their freedoms entirely for granted. I had never been bold enough to enter the campus, but the plastic hospital band that still encircled my wrist was like a magic bracelet that finally allowed me to pass through the iron gates. It reminded me that my life had shifted, that I was no longer myself.

I had wandered the labyrinth of basement corridors, shrinking from the people I passed, sure that, at any moment, I would be identified as an impostor and escorted off the premises. *Rabbi Kaplan's daughter,* the security guard would snarl. *What the hell do you think you're doing here?*

Eventually, I found the small admissions office, filled out a form, tried to find my voice to cough up questions about this mysterious process. At home, I wrote essays and filled out scholarship applications, startled by how simple and doable it all was.

For Yeshivish Jews, higher education was forbidden. This was in contrast to Modern Orthodox Jews and non-Orthodox Jews, who were known for academic achievement. But that brand of Judaism—the Judaism of bagels and lox, "my son the doctor," and Woody Allen—was foreign to me. Scholarship in the Yeshivish community was restricted to Talmudic scholarship and practiced only by men. I'd never dreamed that my education might continue beyond a year or two in seminary, studying Jewish philosophy. Now, applying to college, I was as tense and frightened as if I were trying to hurl my body through a glass wall. Would I lose my love of God if I went to college? Would college pull me further into a spiral of self-destruction? Would I end up lying in the gutter, looking back at this decision with bitter regret?

But when the letter came in the mail, notifying me that I had been accepted and awarded a full scholarship by the president of the college, I whooped with joy and taped the sheet of paper to the fridge. I enrolled as a full-time evening and Sunday student so I could keep my daytime job—my scholarship wouldn't pay my rent. I kissed that letter every day on the way to the shower, as if it were a mezuzah.

Finally, I located James Hall. Inside, there was a line for the elevator. I found the stairs and took them two at a time to the fifth floor. I couldn't be late. I was not going to mess this up by missing a moment of my first class. Searching the doors, I finally found room 5311 tucked around the corner of a hallway. Breathing heavily, I slid into a seat in the front row and looked around.

A man in a beanie cap slouched low at a desk, spinning a pencil on its end. Three girls in the back, each in thigh-sculpting jeans, their breasts spilling out of their tops, laughed loudly, jabbing the air with long pink nails. I took my notebook out of my purse and placed it square in the middle of the desk, pen neatly at its side. I pushed my glasses up my nose and tucked my hair behind my ears.

The clock on the wall said 5:52. Class didn't start until 6:05. Should I risk going to pee? I wondered. I imagined getting locked in a stall, missing my class, being summoned to the registrar, told that I had forfeited my scholarship. *Don't you dare ever show your face on campus again!* I crossed my legs resolutely. No. I had no idea what the rules were in college, or how strict the teachers were, but I wasn't going to do anything that might mess this up.

Slowly, the classroom filled. A man in his thirties, in a suit jacket and jeans, settled himself on the desk at the front of the room.

"I'm Pete Gordon," he said with a relaxed smile. "Let's learn some psychology."

I raised my eyebrows. Would any students dare call him Pete?

"Okeydokey," Professor Gordon said. "How many men do we

have here . . . ?" He counted fourteen with a steady finger. "Write down your answer to this question," he instructed, handing a sheet of paper to each man in the room.

I wondered why Professor Gordon had given the men something to do but not the women. I'd thought secular people believed in equality of the sexes.

"Now then," Professor Gordon said, once the men had put down their pens and he'd collected their papers. "Ladies, I want each of you to tell me your favorite fruit."

His eyes darted around the room until he counted three for apples, eight for blueberries, and two for oranges. I didn't offer that my favorite was the persimmon, the smooth orange fruit I had discovered in Israel. I wasn't sure I could push a word past the carpet in my throat, into the vastness of the room. The professor, collecting answers from my eager classmates, didn't notice my silence.

Professor Gordon rifled through the men's papers, tallying up the responses they had written down.

"Two for bananas, two for apples, one for blackberries, one for pears, one for strawberries, two for watermelon, four for plums"—he chuckled at that—"and one for mangoes." He sketched a quick diagram, mapping out how different the men's and women's preferences were.

"So what do you make of women all choosing similar fruits, the men being so creative?" he asked. The students shouted out suggestions about the nature of men and women.

In ninth grade, Mrs. Lobenberg had taught us that men and women were different, physically, emotionally, and spiritually. "We have different responsibilities," she said. "Neither is better. We each have our role. Men are scholars, but a woman, as she raises her children and supports her husband, has her own wisdom."

But did the men in the class respond with more ideas than the women because they were smarter, I wondered, or was the difference a consequence of the men having been asked the question on paper instead of aloud?

It seemed my observation was correct. Professor Gordon talked about peer pressure and ideas of free will and how perception could be altered by context. For each concept, he cited a study or a scientist, revealing the worlds of academia that lay out there to be discovered. Amazed, I filled pages with blue ink scrawl. I had never realized that non-Jews had such depths of knowledge.

It seemed as if only moments had passed when Professor Gordon stopped, swinging his hand wide and freezing dramatically.

"Seven-thirty," he said, "that's it for me. See you Thursday."

I sat still as my classmates filed out. Only when I was alone could I stand, pick up my purse, and slowly make my way out of the building, home.

My favorite class was Drawing 1, taught by Professor Persichini. Persichini was a thin man with gray hair combed across his head. He wore the same polka-dot cardigan to every class and held his head to the side as he spoke in lilting half-questions, as if he were a teenage girl. He's gay, I realized. This is a gay man. I had never met one before. There were no gay Yeshivish men. His hands were clean, and his smile, when he stopped to look over my shoulder at my drawing of the vase he had set up, seemed genuine.

"Nicely done," he said, tapping my shoulder. I wondered if a gay man's touch counted as a sin.

Halfway through the semester, I arrived at Professor Persichini's class to find a woman in a terry robe standing in place of the usual vase and flowers. I set my pad on the easel as the model took off her robe and her nakedness filled the room.

"A woman's body is so precious it has to stay hidden," my

mother had said many times. "The queen hides her most precious jewels; she doesn't flaunt them."

The model stretched her arms, bent one knee, arched her back in a quick succession of poses as our pencils flew over the paper and we tried to capture the lines of her body.

"Your figure is missing body parts," Professor Persichini said, stopping behind my easel.

I stammered in reply, but he had already moved on to the next student. So I forced myself to stare, to hold my eyes on the woman's body for a full moment. The nipples on the ends of her small breasts looked like pink pennies, her stomach pooched in a soft roll over her generous hips, and a patch of reddish hair guarded her crotch. Finally, I looked at her face. The model was staring at the floor, but her lips were lifted in a half-smile. She didn't seem ashamed at all.

Although I was in college, I still dressed in long skirts and long-sleeved shirts, prayed every morning, and ate only kosher food. I kept the Shabbos, eating peanut butter and jelly sandwiches instead of *cholent* and kugel. I went to work every day. Paid my rent on time. If I was good enough, I hoped, somehow I could make a healthy life for myself. Finish my degree. Get a better job. Find a good man to marry, soon. Despite my diagnosis of PID, find some way to have and raise a bunch of children in a home that was probably more Modern Orthodox than Yeshivish but still kept God and tradition at its core.

None of my efforts impressed my parents. I rarely spoke with them. The only sibling I had much contact with was my brother Elisha. Four years older than me, Elisha was my only older brother. I had vivid memories of my father wielding a knife and chasing Elisha, a curly-headed troublemaker, from the Shabbos table in anger. After his Bar Mitzvah, Elisha was sent away to better yeshivas than Pittsburgh could offer. He lasted only a few months in each one before he was kicked out for escaping through the air ducts after curfew or talking back to a rabbi. While a girl's most important duty was to stay modest, a boy's was to spend long days and nights pondering ancient religious texts. But Elisha was not, as they said, "a good learner." When I had entered adolescence, he had become a confidant. He never sided against our parents, but he was willing to hear me out as I complained about their sternness, their rules. We didn't see each often. Once I left home, we saw each other even less. Still, he had a special place in my heart, and I knew he felt the same about me.

"How are you?" he would ask when he called. "I'm all right," I would say, trying to maintain a brave front. I was loving college, but at the same time, I could not erase the memory of Nicholas from my mind.

I could not forget about the PID. Babies made me cringe. I tensed when I passed pregnant women. But I pushed my worries aside, distracting myself with school. I fought through my calculus sets. I aced my chemistry quizzes. I read Kant till the philosophical mumbo-jumbo phrases fell apart and the meanings became clear. Ah, so our minds shape the information we process. Our realities are limited by our perceptions. Got it.

Struggling to keep up with a full course load of homework while working and juggling a double commute, I had no time for social events at college or even friendships, but there was a guy in my drawing class who always smiled at me. His name was Thomas. He was short, with long hair curling around his face and a sly grin. He often wore a black T-shirt with a cartoon character on it.

"Love your shadowing," he said one Tuesday evening, fists on his hips, looking over my shoulder at my still life of a vase and a baseball. "You're talented, you know?"

"Oh, please," I said, ducking my head. "Your stuff is always incredible."

Professor Persichini's quick hands rearranged the objects in the middle of the room, and as one, we turned to our easels, ripped off the drawings we'd been working on, tossed them to the floor, and began sketching the new arrangement, eyes narrowed, hands swinging up to measure proportions and then back down to the paper to darken a line. We had ten minutes to complete our drawings before the professor would rearrange the composition again, and the first few minutes of a new setup were always a silent frenzy.

At the start of the next class, Thomas claimed the spot next to me, and for the rest of the semester we worked side by side, commenting on each other's sketches, offering suggestions couched in compliments. With Thomas's encouragement, my pencil lines became darker, swifter. They wavered less. I felt a buoyant pride in watching my skill as an artist grow.

Thomas wasn't a big talker, but he did mention a girlfriend and he never seemed to be interested in anything more than our friendly chats. Twice a week, I looked forward to his welcoming smile, to our easy conversation as we worked next to each other.

On the first day of Hanukkah, the late-afternoon sky was porcelain blue, the air bitterly cold. After work, I ran to the subway to squeeze into the rush-hour train that would take me to school. When my chemistry lab ended, I hurried off campus, burying my chin in the collar of my coat, hiding from the biting wind, my breath fogging up my glasses.

Brooklyn College was, ironically, set in the heart of Flatbush, a large Yeshivish community. That night the blocks surrounding the campus glowed with bright windows as family after family gathered in elaborate scenes of festive celebration. Men raised burning candles, and children gathered around silver menorahs. Families danced to songs and music I could not hear. Even with a window, a lawn, and a dark night between us, I could almost smell the aroma of the doughnuts and latkes piled on the dining room tables. I tried to walk faster, but I couldn't escape the scenes of joy. I couldn't stop the memories: my father reciting each word of the candle-lighting blessings distinctly and clearly, the taffy-colored candles I'd jam in my aluminum menorah, the songs we'd sing when the last wick was lit.

The emotions built in my stomach, filling my lungs, cramming my windpipe until I couldn't breathe. I was swallowing hoarse sobs.

I made it home, but my apartment was too small. Too still. Too cold. I blew my nose on a piece of toilet paper, but the tears and the snot kept running. Too much. Too much. Too fucking much. I couldn't hold all the emotion in my body. The pressure was mounting. I needed release. I needed to let it all out.

My pink plastic razor sat on the edge of the bathroom sink. I clenched my fist around it.

Tearing at my sleeve, I pulled the blade against my exposed skin. The anger, the sadness, the confusion—it all roared in my ears as I bit into my flesh.

A pearl of purple blood bloomed on my arm. It rolled across my skin, extending into a trickle, a small river. It looked like a jeweled necklace, bright and precious in the bathroom light.

At the sight of my blood, my tears slowed. I felt a warmth toward the bleeding girl sitting on the toilet.

"Poor Leahchke," I whispered. The sticky trail of blood dripped over my elbow and hit the grimy tiles in red splatters. I put a Band-Aid on the cut and went to do my homework.

The cutting gave me such release, I returned to it again and again in the days that followed, until it became a regular habit. The relief I found in cutting my skin helped me cope as I lived my split life of religion and college, modesty and loneliness, hope and memory. And thanks to my long sleeves, no one saw the railroad of bloody tracks that made their way up and down my arms.

• • •

In the spring, I signed up for Utopian Literature, Acting 101, Biology 101, Drawing 102, and Psychology 101. In acting class, I was partnered with Amina, a plump Palestinian American who looked, with her big brown eyes and tawny skin, like she could have been my sister. Skeptical of both the disgust with Zionism and the hatred of Arabs that I had been raised with, I didn't have many opinions on the Arab-Israeli conflict, but Amina and I still carefully avoided that topic, bonding instead on a common distaste for women's roles in our families and our insistence that we would live our lives differently. She invited me to dinner, but I had class every night of the week. She asked me to see a matinee play with her, but I was glad to say I couldn't make it because I worked during the day. I didn't want to admit that I couldn't afford the ticket.

"Why don't you wear jeans?" she asked me one evening. We had stayed late to rehearse a short skit we'd be performing for the class the following day. "It's a religious thing, right?"

"Yeah," I said. "Pants, short sleeves—none of that is allowed."

"You don't think that's repressive?" she asked. She was lounging on a desk, her feet up on a chair, her chin tilted back, black curls cascading down her back. Unlike me, Amina always looked perfectly at home in her body.

I recrossed my legs. "I don't think so," I said. "Listen, it's not like secular women in their shorts and tank tops are being treated all that well by men."

Amina raised an eyebrow. I could see she had strong opinions on the subject, but she went back to reciting her bit in the sketch, her clear voice filling the classroom.

A few weeks later, Elisha called with the news that he was engaged. I could hear the joy in his voice. I was happy for him. On the day of the ceremony, I put on a borrowed gown and met my family at the wedding hall. We greeted each other with cool cordiality. It was awkward to be among my sisters again— taller, prettier strangers than the last time I had seen them. Still, the tension couldn't eradicate my joy for my older brother. Joy mixed with envy. Elisha would have everything: a wife, babies, the whole world. But what about me? I was ruined. A dirty girl. I might have looked as religious as my sisters, but I would never have a wedding like this. I would never have any future at all.

I danced with the women and grinned till my cheeks hurt. Each time someone grabbed my hand to pull me into a hora, my broken skin, hidden under my velvet sleeves, tingled.

chapter ten

TWO WEEKS LATER I STOOD AGAINST a wall, rocking carefully to the music, watching the crowd, the only white girl in the club. Everybody else was dark and slick in the heat. They danced, throwing their weight from hip to hip, jutting their chins to the rhythm. The women wore magnificent outfits: tiny leather miniskirts pulled around thick thighs, glittery scraps of material draped over opulent breasts. I rolled my long peasant skirt up a little higher and admired how confidently the women shook their shoulders.

The man in front of me stepped backward onto my foot. He turned around.

"Sorry, so sorry." He put a hand on my shoulder, his quick eyes taking in my skin color, my outfit.

"Don't worry," I shouted, pushing my meek voice over the loud music. I was glad for the excuse to have him—to have anyone—talk to me.

The man reminded me of Nicholas. The same long dreadlocks. The same chocolate skin and wiry, hard body, only shorter, just an inch or two taller than me.

"D'you want a beer?" His accent was Brooklyn, not Jamaica.

I hated the taste of beer, but it didn't matter that night. I had earned an A in every one of my classes. Celebrating the completion of a full year of college with a perfect GPA, I was treating myself to one wild night, breaking out of my shell to toast my success in the secular world. I had waited for Shabbos to end, then wandered the dark streets of East Flatbush, my long hair loose, a layer of lipstick thick on my mouth, twenty bucks folded in my sock, walking until I found bright lights and angry music to break up the night. I had never been to a club before, but that's where the goyim went, wasn't it? That's where *frei* bums rocked out, crazy, sexy, free.

I wore a long skirt and a blouse. I didn't have any pants, and even if I had, I would have been too afraid of the neighbors gossiping to wear them in public. I was looking for trouble, but I didn't want anyone to know.

When the man pushed his way back from the bar, he passed me an open bottle that was slippery and cold. The beer tasted like piss. I gulped it down anyway.

"I'm John," he said, squeezing in behind me. He rocked his shoulders to the beat, draping his arm at my waist.

"I can't dance," I screamed back over the music, embarrassed. The only dances I knew were the choreographed group dances of my childhood.

John tried to show me, cupping my hips in his hands, moving them in slow, circular dips to the reggae music. I sucked down the beer until my body melted and I could move without stumbling, resting into John's rhythm and letting his hands take me where they wanted. I followed him to another part of the club, where the music was even louder, the dance floor even more packed. Pushing at me in the haze of alcohol and noise, John's hands bent me forward, so that my cheek was pressed against the sweaty back of the man in front of me. I was tethered to John, but I was swimming.

There was a penis up against my vulva.

I noticed this loosely. Everything was so loud. Everything was so much. John must have maneuvered his penis under my skirt. It was brushing my skin. He pulled at my wavy body, bending me into a half-crouch so he could stick himself into me. I didn't care. Everything was wild. Everything was free. I moved against him. He moved in me. The room hugged me. The drink freed me. All boundaries were lifted. Nothing mattered at all.

In the morning, I woke up feeling as if my brain had thickened into a cement block that knocked around my skull. The taste of horse poop filled my mouth. I stayed in the shower until the water ran cold, leaning my throbbing forehead against the slimy tiles. I imagined throwing a rope over the pipe running across the ceiling, the other end around my neck.

Hideous bitch, I thought, looking into my bloodshot eyes in the mirror. I slapped my face, but the force of the blow was not enough. I grabbed the razor and hacked at my leg, lifting up skin in translucent strips that released streams of blood.

But this time, the anger was stronger than that. The blood brought no release, only more fury.

Dumb fucking bitch. Stupid slut. Fucking pig. I found a bottle of aspirin in the medicine cabinet and wrestled with the cap. I threw two pills to the back of my throat and swallowed them down with a palmful of sink water. The pills left a bitter trail on my tongue. I shook out four more and swallowed them, watching my reflection all the while. Then four more. And four more. The medicine stuffed my throat. My stomach rocked with nausea. You don't deserve to live, I sneered, my reflection wobbly with tears. You're evil. You're gross.

When I cried this deep, all the pain rose into my eyes. All the hurt I normally kept hidden radiated from my flushed face and puffy lips.

The movement of my hand from bottle to mouth seemed lit up, as if by spotlight. All the world was watching. My eyes glinted. My hair trembled, loose and wild around my face. With each handful of carefully counted pills, I became more vibrant.

After I'd swallowed seventy-five aspirin, I had no more room.

The medicine tamped down my anger. Filled with a peaceful serenity, I went to get help.

There was no emergency room for formerly ultra-Orthodox young women who were overwhelmed, confused, lost. But young women with half a bottle of aspirin in their stomachs could go right to the ER.

Outside, it had started to rain. Dark gray spots dappled the cement. I hurried down the block, pushing against the exhaustion that filled my body like wool stuffing. The street was empty. The men of my neighborhood were still in the synagogues, welcoming the Shabbos. Their wives and children were waiting behind platters of food, in the warm safety of their homes.

When I got to the hospital, I told the intake nurse what I had done. My head felt heavy and dense, like a bowling ball wobbling on my neck. "Who is your emergency contact?" the nurse asked. Elisha and his wife had moved to Lakewood, and with my mind slowed by the pills, I could not remember his new number. "A name, please?" the nurse asked sharply. "Becky Kaplan," I finally said and began to give her my parents' number. I stated the area code and the exchange, then paused and made up four random numbers. No matter what happened, I didn't want them to call my mother. I couldn't deal with her, now, too.

The nurses made me strip in the little curtained cubicle in the ER. They took away my clothes and my earrings and gave me a hospital gown and a white piece of fabric that went over my head and was tied to the bed, leaving my hands free but ensuring I could not walk away. "Swallow this," one nurse instructed me, handing over a bottle with a straw.

"What is it?" I whispered.

"Charcoal."

The black liquid was sticky and thick. After one sip, I gagged. I toyed with the straw. The nurse towered over me.

"Drink," she said. "Drink, or we'll have to put a tube down your nose. Would you prefer that?" Her black eyes held no pity.

I took another sip. The stuff coated my throat. It was so thick there was no room for air to escape. Charcoal poured from my mouth and in hot streams out of my nostrils. I lay back in the bed, puddles of black vomit soaking my gown, exhaustion pinning me to the mattress.

At two in the morning I was still in the ER, waiting for a bed in the main ward. The pills weighed my body down and made me feel like I had cotton in my ears. I could barely hear the cries and beeps and pages around me.

A doctor with bushy blond hair stopped by my bed. He felt my wrist for a pulse.

"I can't hear anything," I told him, my own words sounding muffled in my head.

"That's a regular symptom of overdosing," he said briskly as he scribbled a note on my chart. "I'll come back soon to check on it. You shouldn't have overdosed in the first place. There are consequences to your actions."

I tried to roll over onto my stomach, but I was tied to the bed at the waist. I hunched over the bedpan, waiting for the next gush of vomit, waiting for the night to pass.

Later in the evening, I needed to pee. The nurse on duty took his time wandering over to my bed. I squeezed my thighs together in desperation. He was a middle-aged guy with brown shadows across his face. He'd been throwing looks my way all night.

"I need to go to the bathroom," I told him, when he finally came.

"No, no," he said. "You have to use a bedpan. I can't untie you." He passed me a pan and pulled the curtain around my bed. He came back into the cubicle before I was done, catching me perched on the pan full of urine, naked from the waist down. I grabbed at my gown and tried to slide off the pan without spilling the hot pee on the mattress.

He smiled as he took it away. He came back with a wet cloth. Hoisting my grimy body in his arm, my side against his chest, he gently wiped the sweat and guck from my face and neck.

When he lay me back down, I wanted to dig my fingers into his warm skin. I wanted him to keep on holding me. But he left, drawing the curtain behind him. I closed my eyes and put my palms to the places on my hip and shoulder where his hands had held me, as if I could trap the warmth of his touch for just a while longer.

"They're moving you up to the seventh floor," a nurse told me a few hours later.

"What's on the seventh floor?"

"You'll find out soon enough," she said, her eyes down on the chart, her lips twitching.

"It's for the crazies," the cleaning man chimed in, once the nurse had left. "They lie around on the floor all naked, having sex." This was the fourth time he had cleaned around my bed that afternoon. "You don't belong in the psych ward," he told me. "They force medicine down your throat. You're too young and too beautiful—too young for me, though. Don't let them put you there."

I closed my eyes.

I went when they came for me.

I was happy to go.

chapter eleven

MY ROOMMATE MOOED LIKE A COW but moved with the un-
even gait of a camel, jerking her head forward while a shudder
swayed through her spine. Her hair was a mass of bumpy
knots. The first night I watched her reach thick fingers under
her hairline and flip the whole frizzy mess off her head, revealing a bristled gray scalp.

I lay in my cot, the sheet pulled to my chin. The voices of
the nurses drifted from the lit hallway. Every thirty minutes
someone came by the door to check on us, making a mark on a
clipboard. I waited for them. My mind was still and calm. I felt
like I was floating on my back in a long river of darkness. There
you are, I wanted to say each time a head popped around the
door frame, half shadowed, half bright with the glare of the corridor's fluorescent bulbs. There you are. You're still here.

At breakfast, I peeled the cover off an apple juice container and
rested it carefully on the edge of the tray. I drank the juice and
a cup of water and a cup of lemon tea. I'm not going to eat, I
decided. I didn't want to dirty myself with food. I threw out
the meal, still Saran-wrapped, and the juice container and the
two white foam cups, but I held on to the foil juice top, hiding

it in my fist. I loved the calmness and the rules and the safety of the ward, but I wanted more.

With my heart pumping in my throat, I made my way to the largest private bathroom, the one that had a lock. Sitting on the closed toilet, I pulled the edge of the metal top across my upper arm. It made no mark. I tore the foil with my teeth. The ripped edge was sharper. Sawing over and over my skin, I made three thin lines of blood.

For two days, I rolled back my sleeves, immodestly displaying my elbows and arms. No one said a thing. Finally, the old Indian guy throwing lunch trays at us over the counter noticed the cuts.

"Did you do that?" he asked.

I wanted to smile with relief, but I sucked in my gums and shrugged.

"Did you do that here? To yourself?"

"Yeah," I said.

The lunch guy told Dr. Richardson, the head psychiatrist on the ward, who summoned me to his small office for a chat.

"You can call me Hank," he said. He was dark-skinned and short, only a little taller than me in my hospital slippers. He had a square chin like a comic-book hero. We sat facing each other almost knee to knee.

"Let me see, please," he said.

I pulled back the hospital gown's sleeve. Hank's eyes fixed on the cuts I had made over the past few months. He stood up to get a few inches closer to the scabs. I hid my smile, pleased at his attention.

"I see the fresh cuts, but you've obviously done this before. How long have you been cutting yourself?"

"I don't, not very often—I only started a few months ago."

"What do you use?" he asked, scribbling notes in my folder.

"A razor." I worried that he would misunderstand me. "It's not senseless," I said quickly. "It's a coping mechanism. The emotion gets so intense in me, I feel like I'm going to explode. Cutting opens me. Then the emotions can come out. It calms me down. It lets me feel."

As I spoke, I suddenly had a vivid memory of my mother on Friday afternoons, shouting as she scurried about the kitchen, frantic to get the chickens in the oven and the soups on the stove, preparing all the food for that night and the following day, desperate to finish before sunset arrived and all cooking was forbidden.

"Don't talk to me unless you're bleeding!" she would yell.

Will you talk to me now, Mamme? I'm bleeding! Will you talk to me now?

My control crumbled. My shoulders shook as tears slid down my cheeks and dripped off my chin. Hank offered a tissue.

"You know," he said gently, "if you hurt yourself again, we will have to put you under observation. Would you like to be constantly watched, morning and night, like Keo?"

Keo was a moon-faced Japanese girl who wandered the psych ward, asking each guy she encountered, in her high-pitched voice, "Can I suck your cock, motherfucker?"

I pressed my lips together hard, drew my legs into myself, and wrapped my arms around my knees.

I wanted to confess that I wasn't eating, but I kept my mouth shut. I had gotten enough attention. And I didn't want them to force me to eat. The hunger was making my ribs rise and putting sparkles in front of my eyes.

When Hank dismissed me, I went to sit in one of the orange chairs in the dayroom, beside Kevin. Kevin was an Irishman in his twenties with features as open as a child's and clear green eyes that looked into space. He gave off a sour smell like unwashed clothes and sweat.

"What are you thinking, Kevin?" I asked him.

A few minutes later, he shuddered, then muttered something

unintelligible in his thick brogue. He smiled, and the gleam of his teeth made him appear sane.

I sat next to him, staring into space, the earthy smell of my unwashed bra wafting upward. When the nurses and guards left the room, Kevin laid his head on my lap and I ran my fingers through his hair. Together we watched the soap operas and sitcoms that played on the TV, one after another.

Because we were stuck in the alternate reality of the psychiatric ward, I rationalized that it was okay for Kevin's head to rest on my thighs, that this was one episode of female-to-male contact that I wouldn't have to carry around for the rest of my life as another black mark on my soul.

The only interruption to the babble of the TV that afternoon was the distant ringing of the pay phone in the hall. Each time it rang, all heads would swivel, waiting to hear who the call was for. It was never for me.

Likewise, no one came for me from two P.M. to four P.M., when the big TV was turned off and patients sat and spoke in low voices with their visitors. Of course, no one knew I was in the hospital. I had told my boss I had the flu. Still, I managed to be disappointed every day when no familiar face appeared. Each afternoon I was escorted out of the dayroom to wait in the empty cafeteria with the black man who talked to invisible people and the three old ladies, while family and friends were ushered in to the ward to meet with the lucky ones.

I craved the sound of my father's voice. It had been a long time since we had last spoken. Maybe if I called from the hospital, I thought, he'd talk to me. Maybe if I called from the hospital, he'd realize how much I missed him. But I didn't dare. I couldn't risk getting anything other than love. I was too fragile. Instead, five days into my stay, I pieced together Elisha's new phone number and called him.

"I'm in the psych ward," I said. "I tried to kill myself."

There was quiet on the line. I wrapped the silver cord around my finger like a wedding ring, trapping my hand.

"Oh, Leah," he finally said. "Are you okay?"

"Sometimes it's too much," I told him. "Sometimes it's too much to handle."

"I'll always love you," he said. "No matter how many times you mess up. If you're ever——" He searched for the most outrageous possibility. "If you're ever working in a factory, wearing jeans and a T-shirt, I'll still love you."

He asked if I had called our parents. I told him I hadn't.

"Would you like me to call them?" he asked. "Would you want them to come see you?"

My heartbeat quickened. "Of course," I admitted.

That night, the speakers crackled their regular call:

"Medications! Abel, Arnold, Cooper, Chang, Diaz, Froman, Goodman, Kalper, Kaplan, Lopez, Miller, Maldez, Newman, Peterson, Perez, Rothman, Ravine, Sabaretta, Salman, Scott, Smither, Stein, Volio, Wajoski! Medications!"

I had to line up with all the others, but since I'd been admitted voluntarily, I was allowed to refuse the medications each time.

"Don't take the meds," I whispered to Kevin as we waited at the counter. "They only hurt you. They only make pharmaceutical companies rich by numbing people to their problems." My parents had explained it all to me as a child. There was no such thing as mental illness, my mother had taught me. It was all a scam. There was no sorrow a good night's sleep and some prayer couldn't solve.

"I'll hide them, I won't swallow them," Kevin promised with a grin. I watched as he took the pills from the nurse and placed them carefully in his mouth. We ran giggling out of the room, to my bedroom, making sure no one was watching as he slipped inside. Boys weren't allowed in girls' rooms.

I grabbed the small trash can, and he spat the pills out onto the clumps of hair and crumpled tissues. We fell back laughing on my bed. We laughed and laughed, until I began to cry. "Shh, shh," Kevin said. He patted my bony back until the tears left me and my body dried and emptied. We went to the dayroom, back to endless sitting, my empty stomach turning me pleasantly drowsy.

I called Elisha the next morning, as soon as I figured he would be back from morning prayers.

"I spoke to Tatte," he said.

For a moment, my heart filled with relief as I let myself believe that my father might be ready to step in and halt all the madness and return me to the safe embrace of my childhood. Maybe right now he was telling my mother to make up a fresh bed, calling the shul board to say he'd be out of the office for a few days, carrying a balloon and a teddy bear, moving like a steady dot on a map, across the distance between us, coming for me.

"Tatte says you're just doing this for attention," Elisha reported. "He said we need to ignore you."

My tears dribbled down my cheeks and over the rim of the phone. Kevin came to me and put his wiry arms around my stiff body as I hung up with a muffled "Good-bye." I followed him to the alcove by the laundry room, where we had a view of the hallway but were hidden from the nurses and guards.

"Kissy kiss?" Kevin asked, cocking his head to the side, his dreamer's eyes, vacant pools of green, fixed on me. I shook my head no, but I moved close to him, our arms brushing.

Seven days in, I sat in the dayroom with my legs spread wide, shoulders loose, eyes half-closed, mouth half-smiling. They had taken away my clothes when I'd arrived and made me wear a hospital robe. Then they gave me back my clothes and told me I had to wear them again. I didn't want to. I wanted to wear the costume of the sick. Kevin lent me one of his T-shirts. I begged a pair of orderly's pants from the nurse. In real life, I didn't wear immodest pants, but here, it didn't seem to matter. The nothingness of the hours left me lethargic, half-drunk.

The tall Jamaican guard came up to me and made gestures with his hands I didn't understand.

"Huh?" I asked.

"The open beak catches the worm," he said.

"What?"

"You see Brad?" He nodded his head in the direction of the hall. "He's been pacing past that door staring at you and staring at you."

"Doesn't everyone pace? Brad's been pacing for the past week."

The guard looked at my crotch and bit his lip, uncomfortable to have to spell it out. "Shut your legs."

I slammed my knees together, ashamed of my ignorance of pants-wearing etiquette. But still, later that day, when I did my own pacing up and down the hallways of the ward, I relished the wispy kiss of the cotton pants on my thighs, the freedom of my legs as I walked.

The next morning a guy from Hawaii was admitted to the ward. He was gay, it seemed, but still he hugged me and touched me and tapped my shoulder and kissed my cheek. I backed away from his very white mouth until I was up against the wall. Later one of the guards asked if I was finding the new guy intrusive. I was reluctant to be the tattletale, but even more reluctant to be trapped again, so I said yes.

"Bad boy," they rebuked him.

That night, I went away. The Trinidadian guard was on duty, a gentle guy with the build of a football player. He made the half-hourly check on patients, ticking off the names that corresponded to the bodies lying limp across their thin mattresses. I was not in my room, not in the dayroom, not in the TV room, not in the boys' rooms or in any of the beds. The staff members whispered anxiously among themselves, once the guard admitted that one of his charges was missing.

I could see all of this from my position at the far end of the corridor, where I crouched behind the last open door. Peekaboo. My mind was doing curious things, melting and loosening.

The staff members strode through the ward, looking for me. "Leah?" they called. "Does anyone know where Leah is?" "Leah, where are you?" Their voices rose high with worry.

"Here you are," the guard called out, spotting me in my hiding place. His big head bobbed over his scuffed sneakers as he bent down to give me a hand.

"I found her!" he yelled. I didn't mind. I had gotten what I needed. I let him usher me back to my room, a giant paw on my back.

After ten days and as many arguments with Hank about my refusal to take medication, I was released. I signed my papers and hugged Kevin good-bye.

The nurses buzzed me out of the heavy ward doors. I pressed the button for the elevator. As I stood in the narrow corridor, I was gripped by an urge to turn around, to bang on the doors until they let me back in. I wanted to stay where everything was sterile and clean and safe. Where I could be a child. Where people would look after me.

The elevator dinged. The door opened. I stepped inside the empty car. As the elevator sank, the heaviness of reality piled back onto me. Outside, I blinked in the harsh sunlight. The quiet street seemed enormous. I headed home.

My apartment, that night, sounded strangely quiet. The musty smell seemed stronger than usual. I lay in bed until nighttime came. Eventually, I fell asleep. In the morning, I would return to work, to my normal routine.

chapter twelve

I HAD BEEN OUT OF THE HOSPITAL for one month. Then two. Every night, I begged God to send his salvation. I knew that if I found a good guy, a religious guy, who wanted to marry me, then everything would fall into place, like a righted train clicking back into its tracks.

Three weeks before the fall semester began, Elisha called. He had someone for me, he said. He could set me up. A swell of relief rose in my chest. It's over. This whole fucki—stupid nightmare is over, I thought. If Elisha had someone for me, maybe God was ready to perform a miracle and redeem me, turn me back into the girl I'd once been, erase my recent past in a swooping gesture of divine magnanimity.

I pulled the phone cord across the apartment and sank onto my bed.

"His name is Duvi Beigelstock," my brother said. "We were in yeshiva together in Chicago, a few years back. I don't know him well, but I heard he's looking."

"What do you know about him?" What's wrong with him, was what I meant. What major handicap did this Duvi have that would make Elisha think he would be an appropriate match for me?

"He comes from a good home," Elisha said. "But he went off as a teenager."

That's what they said about people like me: we were "off the path." If a boy wore a blue shirt instead of a white shirt, or a girl wore long earrings or outlandishly short hair, they might be labeled "modern," but if a girl kissed a boy or broke the Shabbos, she was "off the path." The very phrase reeked of disdain. These were pathetic people. Without religion, their lives crumbled.

"Duvi was an addict," Elisha said. "Cocaine, I think. He's intense, very smart, a lot of personality—a *chevraman*. My sense is, he's a very spiritual kind of guy."

That sounded like everything I was looking for, except the cocaine addiction. But who was I to judge a weakness of the flesh? Perhaps it would help him overlook my sins.

When I said my prayers that night, I scrunched my eyes shut and begged that this man would be the one for me. I was nineteen years old, about to be twenty. I had almost every card stacked against me. If I got any older, my slim chance of getting married would evaporate altogether.

Of course, there was the issue of my fertility. My doctor had told me there would be no way to know the damage caused by the PID until I tried getting pregnant. But I didn't let myself dwell on that problem. This is a miracle, I thought. Duvi might be a miracle. This is God proving his mightiness, and he will smooth the path, reverse the past, save me entirely.

The evening of my date, I committed to the ordeal of blow-drying my hair straight, which was the style for religious girls. The process took an hour; I stood in my claustrophobic bathroom, working the round brush around my head in sections, burning my scalp and yanking the hair dryer down to the tips of my hair until each section lay smooth. When I was done, I swiped the sweat off my neck, wishing I could jump back into the shower to rinse off all over again.

I had skipped lunch each of the four days since Elisha had called, and I was thrilled to find that I could now squeeze into my old blue Sabbath suit, the nicest thing I owned. I picked through my eclectic makeup kit, brushing on some eye shadow, wiping it off, reapplying a different color.

The doorbell rang at seven. I was ready, waiting on the other side of the door, counting ten Mississippis before I answered.

There he was, Duvi Beigelstock.

I had been told that he was good-looking, but the fuzzy mental image of a yeshiva boy did not match the man standing in front of me: tall, broad-shouldered, with the icy blue eyes and easy bearing of an Abercrombie & Fitch model. His dark suit was crisp and fit him well, his tie was not too thin and not too wide, his thick hair curled around his black velvet yarmulke. He looked at me silently for a long moment.

"Hi," he finally said.

"Hi."

He smiled, his full lips lifting with a hint of mischief. "It's nice to meet you." He moved back as I stepped into the driveway beside him.

"You, too," I whispered, a little awed by his unexpected beauty.

My heels clicked on the pavement. A light breeze lifted my hair off my shoulders as we made our way down the street, careful that we didn't accidentally brush up against each other.

"I thought we could go for sushi," he said. "The place on Avenue J."

If we were more strictly observant, Duvi would have taken me to sit in a hotel lobby to talk over Cokes. A bustling hotel lobby ensured that you wouldn't be alone, tempting physical hungers, but it was also likely that you wouldn't be seen and gossiped about (even a boy and girl on an arranged date needed to treat their encounter with modesty). Dinner, with the opening of the mouth, the inserting of food, the working of the jaw—that full display of hunger and consumption—was less

modest than sipping a soft drink in a lobby, but it was still a
fair choice for a first meeting.

"Sushi sounds nice." Kosher sushi had recently become a
fad in the religious world. I had passed the Japanese-inspired
place he had in mind but had never been inside.

"So, have you lived in this area for a long time?" Duvi
looked over at me, his eyes connecting with mine, sticking for a
second too long.

We made it through that awkward first bit of conversation,
until we were in the restaurant. He removed his suit jacket and
tossed it over the back of his chair. We looked at the menu and
placed our orders. When the waitress left, Duvi sat still, watching me. The silence unnerved me, but I didn't want to be immodest and jump in with too many questions. I didn't want to
ask him about his parents or his yeshiva, anyhow. I wanted to
know him. I wanted to sink my teeth into who he was. He certainly was no ordinary yeshiva boy.

"So," he said. He looked down at his clasped hands, then
back at me, with a sudden somberness. The twinkling mask
had been wiped away. "I'm sure they told you about me. You
aren't scared?"

The directness of his question floored me.

"I'm not afraid," I said softly, leaning forward. "I think you
can't really love God if you haven't turned your back on him
first."

He nodded. "That is so true. There's a purity now, a hunger
for God, that I never felt before."

"What was before?"

"How much do you want to know?"

"Everything."

Over raw salmon and tuna, he told me about his youth in
yeshiva, his devotion to God as a child, his adolescent rebel-
lions, his transgressions.

"I got into speedballs—do you know what those are?"

I shook my head.

"Crack and speed, basically. I needed the drug—it ruled my life. I did whatever it took to get it. My parents kicked me out, I stole from them, I stole from everyone. Seven hundred dollars from my sister—I took her ATM card and emptied her bank account. I did whatever it took."

He readjusted his yarmulke, pursed his lips as if to stop himself from admitting more. Then he flashed his eyes up at me. "At one point I sold myself, a few minutes in the park with other men, to get the money."

I recognized the hint of pride in his admission. I understood that secret delight in one's ability to be so staggeringly wicked. I had, a few times, experienced that same feeling about my own history.

The depravity of Duvi's past dazzled me. I was flattered and impressed that he was bold enough to defy convention and speak to me of his sordid history at a kosher restaurant on Avenue J, surrounded by bearded men and their bewigged wives and numerous offspring. We belonged to a secret club, the two of us, and he was trusting me with the password.

"You know how they say a holy man falls seven times and gets back up?" he asked, quoting the Hebrew phrase, the ancient words flying smoothly off his tongue. I nodded.

"I always think that it isn't the persistence that makes him holy but the fact that he fell." His eyes sparkled with passion as he spoke. "You can't really commit to being religious, to loving God, if you haven't spent some time with your face in the dirt."

"There are so many things like that," I interjected. "Old teachings that get new meanings when you've experienced certain things."

"Yes, I know," he agreed. "But tell me what you think about." He wanted to know. He really wanted to know what I thought. When had a religious man—any man—ever cared about what I thought?

"Well." My throat closed; I felt suddenly shy. I forced the words out: "Well, like the Shema prayer, everyone says it a million times, right?" He nodded, leaning in eagerly to hear me better. "But what does it actually mean? 'God, our God, is one'? What does that even mean?"

This was something I had thought about often, clinging to the words of that bedtime prayer as if it were a life raft on so many dark nights.

"Yeah," he said. "That's true—it's kind of a strange thing to repeat so often. What do you think it means?"

"Well, that our hungers, at the bottom, no matter who we are or what we desire, our hungers all come from a common, singular desire for closeness to the divine. 'Our God' is all the same one thing. It can become diluted or whatever, or people think they want other things—even drugs, right? Or alcohol or relationships. Or—" I wasn't sure if I could say the word but decided to go for it: "Sex. But really, underneath it all, it's a hunger for our original sustenance, to return to the source of all of life and all of creation. 'God' is 'our God'—it's the same in all of us, and no matter how twisted, it's an echo of our heavenly Father."

"Wow." Duvi shook his head and closed his eyes. "Wow, let me think about that for a moment. Wow. That's really deep."

The waitress had been hovering for a while. She darted forward during that moment of silence.

"Um, we're closing soon, so, you know ..." She gestured to the check, which had been sitting, ignored, on the table.

I looked at the time, startled. It was already ten o'clock.

During our slow walk home, I told Duvi about how I had always been devout but had become distracted by Naftali, how my parents had cut me off, how I had lost my virginity to Nicholas. I boldly savored my description of Nicholas, a dreadlocked Rastafarian, flaunting my own sinful achievements. I told him how I longed to start a family, to find a partner who would understand all the different parts of me, and how together we would build a home devoted to God.

The home I dreamed of wouldn't be as strict and cold as my parents'. I would finish college and get a professional job, but I would also have many children and elaborate Shabbos dinners, and the love between my husband and me would flourish within the boundaries of Jewish marital law. I was sure that with the devoted attentions of a godly man I would never again succumb to my crazy, sinful appetites.

"I want to have a big, open house," I told him. "I always dreamed of that. Tons of guests, all the time, you know?"

He nodded. "It's what I've always dreamed of, too."

We were lingering at my front door. It was late. The street was dark and quiet behind us.

"I should go," he said. I could see, from how his eyes softened, that he wanted to kiss me. I wish I could kiss you, too, I thought. But we'd awakened a purity in each other, a childlike yearning to connect with a force more powerful than any physical urge. The law forbade physical contact, so even though we had both sinned in the past, we parted with a chaste good night.

chapter thirteen

WHEN THE KNOCK CAME THE NEXT EVENING, I ran up the short flight of stairs to the door of my basement apartment. I was wearing a navy skirt and a silky white blouse. My hair was again blow-dried straight and parted on one side. I wore contact lenses and small gold earrings and a thin application of eyeliner that brought out my eyes.

"Hi."

"Hi."

Already Duvi's tall, cocky stance and crooked smile seemed familiar.

"Let just—me just sw—grab a sweater." The words tumbled out of my mouth, garbled and incoherent. Cool it, girl, I thought, swinging around to head back down. Turning too quickly, I tripped over my own feet and toppled down the stairs, landing in a pile on the floor. The burning humiliation could have incinerated me on the spot.

"Are you okay?" Duvi ran down the stairs to crouch over me, his shiny black shoes inches from my fingers. He would not, could not, touch me, but his body was so close, I could smell the clean spice of his skin radiating from the open collar of his white shirt.

I struggled to my feet. Straightened my skirt.

"I—I'm fine." I grabbed my sweater, my eyes watering

with embarrassment. But the magic of his eyes, of our connection as we walked through Brooklyn, wiped away my shame.

We saw each other again the next night. We talked of the true meaning of the concept of the Messiah and the relationship between veganism, macrobiotics, and the laws of kosher.

"Achas shoalti me'eis HaShem," he sang, quoting the familiar psalm as we strolled through the dark streets. "I have one request of the Lord, that which I seek. To dwell in the house of the Lord, all the days of my life. To bask in the sweetness of the Lord and to visit within his sanctuary." He stopped walking and held my eyes as he sang the words *achas shoalti* over and over again. *"I have one request ... I have one request ..."* Overcome, I had to look away.

On the one-week anniversary of our first date, I was hunting for my keys, which had disappeared five minutes before Duvi knocked. He waited inside my apartment, surveying the mess with a bemused smile. After that, he always came inside when he picked me up for our nightly date. He started lingering a little before we went out. We chatted, sitting on the floor because I had only one chair. A man was not allowed to be alone in a room with a woman, but we were too wrapped up in the spiritual ecstasy of our companionship to care.

"You shouldn't leave all this cash lying around," he said to me on our ninth date in eleven nights, his fingers skimming over the crumpled bills scattered on the kitchen table. My apartment was littered with money. Dollars and coins lay across the floor, the furniture, peppering the piles of clothing and the boxes and books that filled the place. When I needed money for something, I scooped my hand across the room and found what I wanted. I had gotten a raise and now earned twenty-five thousand dollars a year, which felt like an enormous amount. I enjoyed treating money like trash, proving my freedom from the grip of poverty, of no longer having to count every penny.

"Why?" I asked.

"I'm an addict," he said. "I'm still an addict, and money lying around triggers me."

The thrill of danger electrified us. His easy admission of guilt
made me feel that I could be my whole self with him, unashamed.

For our eleventh date, Duvi invited me to come to his Nar-
cotics Anonymous meeting. It was held in a church basement
on Avenue N. I sat on a metal folding chair beside him, my jaw
rigid with nerves, sure that I stuck out as a voyeur. Duvi,
clutching a cup of the same black coffee everyone else held,
waved and called hello to the people he knew. The cavernous
room stank of cigarettes. I loved that Duvi was so pure yet still
connected to the sexy indiscretions of his past, to this circle of
dog-eyed men and women who held hands and asked for the
wisdom to know the difference between the things they could
change and the things they must accept.

Sixteen days after we first met, Duvi was at my apartment,
sitting on the floor beside me, his guitar resting on his crossed
legs, playing a slow melody that soon slowed even further, until only one finger was pulling the occasional string, punctuat-
ing long silences.

He was watching me with those clear blue eyes. Watching
me sit with my back against the wall, legs folded up against
my breasts, chin resting on my knees as I gazed at him, following his finger nuzzling the guitar string, sending goose bumps
of desire over my skin.

No, I thought. Please, dear God, I beg you, please don't let it
happen.

I knew what the silence meant. I knew Duvi well enough
by then. He was going to ask me to marry him.

A very tiny piece of my brain retained some sanity in the rush
of relief that Duvi had swept into my life. I knew he was my
beshert, the one man God had declared for me, forty days before
my birth. The one man I had been waiting for all of my life. But I
also know it was too early for us to admit it to each other.

Yeshivish people got engaged after six or eight dates over a period of a few weeks. According to the way things were usually done, we had spent enough time together. But we were not regular people. We needed more time. We needed to slow down, just a little, to get to know each other beyond our shared certainty that we were the reciprocal halves of each other's souls.

Please, God, I begged. Please let him wait.

"Leah," Duvi said softly. My stomach squeezed hard.

"Will you marry me, Leah?" The words hung in the air. I couldn't risk losing my shot at redemption. I nodded, a small jerky motion.

"Yes," I whispered. We smiled at each other. I wanted to fall across the few inches between us and bury my uncertainty up against his chest. But we still couldn't touch. Until we were married, it would not be allowed.

"Let's go outside," he said.

The street was quiet. The windows in the neighboring homes were dark. A garbage truck rumbled past. There was nothing more to say. I had been waiting for this moment all of my life. I am going to be married, I thought, trying to muster up the excitement I believed I should feel, but it was all strangely anticlimactic. I'd thought this happy ending would transform me somehow, instantly make me into someone more holy, more beautiful than who I was. But I was still inhabiting my familiar body. I still felt like myself.

We agreed to keep the engagement a secret for a little while. We would wait until enough days had passed that we could convince our families that this was a godly connection, not just another incident of impulse and desire, like those for which we had both been frequently judged in the past.

I kept a small photo of Duvi beside my computer at work. I got a thrill each time I glanced at his mischievous grin. This is my man, I thought. My *chusson*. Finally, my future is settled and secure.

Sometimes I thought of his large confident hands, his smooth fair skin, wondering what it would feel like to touch him. To be touched by him. Wondering how the union of bodies in holy hunger might be different from the rushed, guilty fumblings of my past.

We spent every free minute together. One Sunday evening we took the train to Manhattan. We walked around Union Square, enjoying the subtle brushing together of our coats. We chatted excitedly about the future. Whether or not we wanted to move to Israel. How much we scorned the materialism of other young married couples we knew. On the train back, I collapsed into the plastic seat next to him, exhausted. I felt so intensely around him that prolonged exposure left me limp.

At Canal Street, an Israeli couple boarded the train, laughing and joking in Hebrew, the woman in jeans, the man bareheaded.

Duvi swung himself up with a big smile, ready to go over to them, then saw me slumped in my seat.

"You don't—?"

I looked at him, hoping it wouldn't be a big deal.

"We should go talk with them, be *mekarev*." To be *mekarev* was to bring someone closer to God. The desire to reach out to this couple exuded from him; his natural charisma would make it easy for him to draw people into his confidence.

"I'm sorry, I can't . . . I'm not like that." It embarrassed me. I wasn't bold enough to strike up a conversation with strangers.

Duvi sat back down, his lower lip in a slight pout. I could see doubt flicker across his face. Was he, an extrovert, so full of joy, so quick to connect with others, going to be stuck for his entire life with someone who was so shy? I felt his disappointment. We rode the rest of the way in silence.

When I got home, the red light on my phone was blinking. I dialed my voice mail.

"Leah, It's Elisha. I just wanted to let you know: *Bubbeh* Rachel passed away. Blessed is the true Judge."

Bubbeh Rachel was my step-grandmother; she'd married my father's father, *Zeide* Chananya, after his first wife died. A stiff, simple woman, she had always been kind to me. When I hung up the phone, I was crying. I picked up the receiver again.

"Duvi," I sobbed. "Will you come?"

He arrived soon enough that the tears still flowed easily, the news still fresh. We talked, the air taut between us. Finally, his arms reached around my shoulders and we touched for the first time. His hold was comforting and warm, like a mother's womb. It terrified me.

"No, no, we can't do this. This is wrong." I drew back. He pulled me close.

As if in a dream, our clothes came off and we tumbled, naked, to my bed, consuming each other's flesh, devouring each other's bodies. His briny skin flipped over and under me, his hot breath on my shoulder. "Oh, God," I cried into his neck. "Oh, God." I had snatched moments of pleasure in sex before, but never had I been subsumed by it like this. Never had I let go so completely.

When Duvi finished, he lit a cigarette and blew the smoke, like a kiss, out the window. Then he left.

God will forgive us, I tried to convince myself. We'll be having sex together for the rest of our lives. One little extra session before we're married will hardly mean anything in twenty years.

It took seven more days for Duvi to break off the engagement. His rabbi had urged him to do so, he told me. His rabbi thought we were too unstable. I knew he kept no secrets from this man, who had helped him rediscover God in his recovery.

I wasn't upset. My heart was filled with trust. It's the right thing, I thought. We are too volatile. Whatever Duvi says, I told myself, is the right thing to do. I believed in him and with my renewed faith in God; I believed heaven was keeping an eye on the two of us. A graceful stillness settled over my thoughts, keeping me calm.

That Saturday night, Duvi knocked on my door. We talked. He reached for me, tried to lift my shirt.

"No," I said. "No, Duvi, no." I stepped back. We had no covenant anymore, no promise of marriage. "No, I can't." Slowly, I closed the door between us.

A few days later, he called, wild, desperate.

"I'm going to crash," he gasped. "The drugs are calling me—I'm going to use."

"Come come come, hold on, just come be with me," I begged. I needed to save him.

He stumbled down the stairs into my apartment, reeking of alcohol. I gave him my body as he wished, in the hope that it would stave off the drugs. I still loved him with everything I had. I didn't want him to hurt himself. And maybe, I reasoned, if I saved him, he'd remember again that I was the one for him.

But this time together, I was reduced to Duvi's vessel. There was no joy in his touch. There was no pleasure in our union. It was the same as it had been with Nicholas. My body felt dirty and numb.

When the man I'd thought I would marry left, after he'd gotten what he wanted, my heart—my calm, cool, God-filled heart—shattered. In the shower, I sobbed as I washed his residue out of me. I scraped my nails across my thighs. Why, I screamed at myself. Stupid idiot. Why did you let him? You think there's some invisible man in the sky protecting you? You're just an ugly slut who's infertile. Who did you think you were fooling?

The pain was too big. My razor lay on the top shelf of my medicine cabinet. I grabbed at it, desperate for its sweet release. The blade went smoothly across my arm, slicing cleanly. Limp with relief, I stood in the shower and watched the streams of blood drip off my body to the bottom of the tub, where they mixed with the water in marbled red currents that spun around the drain.

chapter fourteen

MY BELIEF IN AN ALL-POWERFUL GOD had weakened over time, and this last episode of hopes raised and dashed was too much for it to bear. My relationship with Duvi was a grand finale of religious devotion. After him, there was only silence.

Over the course of the next year, as my heart healed, my observance fell away. Bored on a Saturday, I walked to a distant subway station to avoid the accusing stares of my Jewish neighbors and took the train to explore Manhattan. There was no guilt as I stepped into the car, violating Shabbos. I felt relief in acknowledging the choice I had been edging closer to.

I entered casual relationships with men I met at school, in coffee shops, in the park. I wore new jeans under long skirts, which I removed in the bathroom at college. I ate nonkosher pizza in the cafeteria. With some excitement, I tried bacon. The salty treat was alien and delicious, but not as thrilling as I'd hoped. Whoever God was, I didn't think he'd care much about a young woman gulping down a dinner of pig instead of cow between classes. If there was a God, I thought he'd be less likely to criticize my palate and more likely to praise my tenacity: I had gotten another set of straight A's, maintaining my perfect GPA.

I was still living in a basement apartment on the edges of religious society. Even as I lost my faith, I couldn't figure out how to cross the geographical boundaries of my community. It seemed impossible. Like: how would you get from Dallas to Anchorage on a jar of peanut oil and a paper airplane? The mind cannot organize coherently around the incomprehensible. Despite my changes, it was impossible for me to imagine myself traversing the bridge to a fully secular life.

Max was the one who got me to move. I met Max at a café in the Village, a few months after my twenty-first birthday. He was a short, bald, fifty-four-year-old man with piercing green eyes. I adored him for his definitiveness, his stiff dignity. We saw each other occasionally. After we had sex, he would drive me around Manhattan in his BMW, slipping a Beethoven disc into the CD player. I would lie with the seat back, my eyes closed, letting the sounds ripple over my body.

"You need to move out of this neighborhood," he said one night, after I'd snuck him into my apartment. I had to time the entrance of my lovers to avoid the prying eyes of my religious landlord, who would have exploded if she'd caught me with a man. "How are you going to become your own person?" Max asked. "You can't grow if you're stuck here, in this religious world."

It turned out that all I needed was Max's permission. The new, wholly secular me was fully formed, just waiting for some authoritative man to allow me to reveal it. Before the month was up, I had cleared out of my home, leaving a trash bag of modest skirts and prayer books resting on the curb.

My new place was in Williamsburg, in an old factory that had been converted into lofts connected by halls and dark stairways that reeked of piss. A male model, three musicians, a yoga teacher, two robotics engineers/furniture movers, and a filmmaker lived on my floor. We shared three toilets and two shower stalls and a sink. There was no kitchen. Some days the whole thing felt like summer camp.

I rented an enclosed loft bed in a small apartment. The apartment was divided across the middle by a wall. Jason Davis, a tall glam rock drummer, had a loft bed opposite mine, while Blaze Vincent, a scrawny British rocker, lived behind the wall, in the half of the room with the window. Jason and Blaze were nice to me, but I was too intimidated by their leather jackets and rockstar swagger to develop a real friendship with either of them.

Living among non-Jews, I found the courage to change my wardrobe. I replaced my work skirts with trousers. I flashed my elbows at the world. Many of my colleagues were as religious as my boss. Conversations hushed and stares lengthened when I came into the office, but I kept my head down and stayed focused on my job.

Although my clothing was no longer modest, I still adhered to a professional dress code at work. But on the weekends, I wore an old hip-hop T-shirt Nicholas had left at my house years before, as a shirtdress. I bared my shoulders in tank tops, my thighs in shorts, my toes in sandals. Feeling gloriously free, I flaunted the scars on my arm. I revealed the tops of my breasts. With some embarrassment and some pride, I collected the whistles and stares of passing men like a bouquet of flowers pardoning all the rejection I had ever encountered.

I hadn't overcome my prejudice against television, but I listened to the radio and went to the movies and watched my hipster neighbors, always taking mental notes on how to adjust my posture, my ideas, my presentation so I could better fit into my new world. The more I learned, the more it became obvious to me how little I knew, how different I was from all the men and women around me, whose parents seemed loving, whose spiritual paths seemed simple, whose lives seemed untroubled.

One afternoon I admitted to Blaze that I didn't know any Beatles songs. He invited me to his room to hear a vintage Beatles record. We lay side by side on his mattress and listened to the childish tunes.

Blaze's walls were draped in velvet cloth and tassels. His mattress was ringed with crates arranged with old records and books. He had a little stage set up with drums and a couple of guitars. The air was soupy with grayish light from the window, and the whole space had the artfulness of a movie set.

I lolled my head back off the mattress, my hair pooling on the rug, trying on a casual cool that my pounding heart betrayed.

"What do you want to hear next?" Blaze asked, rolling up to change the record. His platinum hair floated around his face, and his plump lips were startlingly pink against his pale, sunken cheeks. He looked like an angel.

I racked my brain. I didn't want to suggest something stupid, but I didn't know enough to distinguish between songs that were cool and not.

"How about that one with horses—wild horses?" I had heard that song on the radio. I liked it: the imagery of wild horses, galloping free.

"Rolling Stones. I don't have that record. But I'll play it for you if you like."

There was a gentleness about Blaze—as if he had been broken by life and through the cracks of his cool, rock-star shell one could see glimpses of the sweet child inside.

He sat on the edge of the bed and picked at the strings of his guitar, his thin, strong voice sending tingles up my spine.

"You're amazing," I said when he finished. "That was gorgeous."

"Thanks," he laughed. He lay back down on the bed. We stayed that way, in the quiet, for a few moments. I wondered if he wanted me to leave, if the silence was a signal I failed to understand. I moved like a blindfolded woman in this secular world.

"Kiss?" He turned to me, offering his lips. Startled, I pulled back. As soon as I moved away, I regretted it. But then Blaze sat up and said he needed to get to work. I left. He never asked again, and he gently rebuffed my awkward advances.

One evening, a few months later, just as I came in from work, Blaze wandered into the loft shirtless, ribs poking out of his little-boy chest.

"I don't know if I'm going to be here," he said.

Jason was making his first descent of the day from his crate. He wore a leopard-print robe tied around his tall, thin body, straggly chest hair sprouting at the neck. Without his eyeliner, he looked unnervingly like a suburban plumber.

Blaze scratched his hair.

"We might have to leave the apartment—I might have to go back to England."

"Green card?" Jason asked.

Blaze nodded. "Unless I get married." He gave a wry little laugh.

"I'll marry you," I said. The words fell out of my mouth. Like one of Pavlov's dogs: a man had a problem, I leapt to offer the solution. I didn't think through the elaborate commitment, the potential consequences of lying to the government, the emotional impact of being married to a man who was not mine.

"Seriously?" Blaze gave me a skeptical look that didn't entirely hide his hopefulness.

"Sure, why not?"

"No, it's a big deal," he said, turning away and dismissing me with a laugh.

"Seriously, I'll do it."

What do I care, I thought. Chalk one more up for life adventures.

I always thought I'd be married at eighteen, but there I was, almost twenty-two, with nobody. Where I came from, if a girl was still single by twenty-two, she had to be suffering from cystic acne or cancer or divorced parents. I was an old maid, and with whatever damage the PID had done to my fertility, I was sure nobody would ever want to marry me for love. I was too broken. My parents, Naftali, Jacob, Nicholas, Duvi—they had all taught me that I was unlovable.

Once it sank in that I was going to marry this man, at least on paper, I was excited to realize that there was something in this arrangement for me as well. If Blaze became my husband, I could take his name. Throughout my childhood, I had been Rabbi Kaplan's daughter. One of the Kaplan girls. A descendant of the rabbinic Kaplan family. Now every time someone said my full name, I was reminded of my father and the world I had lost. With Blaze's help, I could become Leah Vincent, a woman without a history.

I had dreamed of my wedding thousands of times. I had fantasized about Rabbi Shmuel Kamenetsky and Rabbi Matisyahu Salomon reciting the blessings in their trembling voices, my mother at my elbow, my father beside my groom, smiling with love, hundreds of people crowded in rows, witnessing the commencement of my grown-up life.

The reality was a perversion of that image. No rabbi. No family. No wedding guests. The married filmmaker from down the hall, a woman Blaze pretended he wasn't having an affair with, was our witness. Instead of a billowing gown, I wore black pants, black stiletto boots that laced up the front, and a black top that displayed my cleavage.

After Blaze and I recited our vows, the officiator declared that we could kiss each other. She had a wrinkle in her nose, as if she, for one, wasn't being fooled. Blaze leaned over and kissed me lightly and then stuck his tongue inside the filmmaker's mouth.

When I next saw Max, that declarative lover who had convinced me to live in a goyish neighborhood, he was not pleased with the whole affair.

"You did what? You're living where?" he exclaimed. When I admitted that I paid Blaze four hundred and fifty dollars a month in rent and slept on a blanket in a crate that hung from the ceiling, he became incensed.

"This fucker is ripping you off—you don't even have a mattress, and he got you to marry him? That's ridiculous!"

I tried to explain that I had offered to marry Blaze, but Max wasn't convinced. I quickly let his narrative take over. Yes, I was the victim. I had been conned.

Now each time I saw Blaze, my mind churned with regret. The reality of our legal status weighed on me. It was not the inconsequential simple thing I'd thought it would be. Blaze was expecting me to lie for him so he could get his green card. I hated to lie—and I was terrible at it when I tried. I grew ever more tense, imagining the untruths I'd have to recite at the immigration interviews.

I was also experiencing an unexpected emotional backlash. I was finally somebody's wife—but my husband meant nothing to me. My husband was a man who was barely my friend. A man who maybe was taking advantage of me. I couldn't look this grotesque dream in the face every day.

I ran.

Four weeks after the wedding, I found a studio apartment in Prospect Heights. It had a leaky fridge and a window that looked onto a brick wall.

I didn't want to talk to Blaze. I was too confused, unsure of whether or not he had used me. Our marriage certificate sat in my suitcase. Despite the stress of abandoning him, I still proudly wielded his goyish name. Vincent. It sounded right, as if it had always been mine alone.

• • •

My new building was filled with college students. Creative types. I saw them as I trudged to and from classes and work. The girls wore tight jeans and oversized tops; with loose, lush hair framing their radiant faces, they teetered on high heels as they squeezed past me in the hallway. The guys carried their bikes up the stairs on their slender backs, fedoras balanced on their heads.

In Williamsburg I had been an excited immigrant, confident that I'd soon assimilate. But now, ashamed by my failed marriage, I felt my confidence wane. I did not know a way into this carefree group. I felt disfigured by my past, my strange journey, which had left me old and weary in some ways, and as ignorant as a baby in others.

One evening in the beginning of December, a few weeks after I'd moved, I was walking off campus when I ran into Thomas, my old friend from art class. I hadn't seen him since my first semester, but I recognized that mischievous smile in an instant.

"Thomas! Oh my God!"

We hugged and caught up on classes and life, our breath releasing in white puffs of air. I asked after his girlfriend. He commented on my jeans. When he had known me, I had worn only skirts.

"It's freezing," I finally said, my teeth chattering in the cold. "I'm going to grab dinner at this pizza place—wanna come?"

I didn't want to let go of the joy of seeing someone I used to know. I wanted to prolong the feeling of connection. As we ate, sitting side by side on stools, Thomas spoke fondly of his girl-friend, but his eyes lingered on my breasts, my thighs, my face. Under his gaze, I felt my limbs surge with a new, powerful grace.

"You've got some sauce—here—" Boldly, I dabbed at a fleck

of tomato sauce on his chin with a napkin. His eyes went still. The air between us grew tense with electricity.

"Can I come back to your place?" he asked, pressing his knee lightly against mine.

"Yes," I said. My voice came out husky and low.

When we got to my apartment in Prospect Heights, his hands were everywhere. "You're gorgeous," he moaned. "Oh my God, your skin feels incredible." The sex was quick, intense, like a wave peaking. When he was done, he went to the bathroom to wash up.

"I gotta go," he mumbled, not meeting my gaze as he grabbed his jacket from the floor.

When I closed the door behind him, I was sure that my desire had destroyed whatever friendship we might have had.

When my twenty-second birthday arrived, there was nobody to celebrate with. I took the train to Union Square and walked into the first dark bar I found. It was filled with young people watching sports on overhead televisions and screaming their flirtations at each other. I had never been to a bar, but I didn't want to be alone on my birthday, and this "first" seemed appropriate for the occasion.

"Can I order an apple martini please," I shouted at the bartender, when I finally got his attention. I had once read a murder mystery in which the dashing female detective always ordered apple martinis.

The fluorescent green drink was surprisingly bitter. I drank it quickly. The second one was sweeter, milder. The room gained a nice rhythm, and I began to feel comfortable. The bartender had stepped out into the crowd, and suddenly he was behind my barstool, with a hand on my shoulder, leaning toward me.

"Your undies are showing," he shouted into my ear, in a clipped Irish brogue. I looked behind my back as he walked away. My thong was peeking over my low-cut jeans. I pushed my underwear down into my pants and laughed.

"I'll take another one," I shouted, when I caught the bartender's eye again. The music was loud, and I liked it.

"You're sure you're not going too fast?" he asked me as he poured the third martini. His long and elegant fingers slid up and down the icy martini shaker.

"It's my birthday," I shouted. "And I'm miserable, so I want to drink." He smiled at me, and I put a five-dollar tip for the ten-dollar drink on the bar. I was spending my grocery budget down to the last penny.

"What's your name?" he asked, his hazel eyes gleaming. I loved his accent.

"Leah. What's yours?"

Before he could answer, he was called to the end of the bar by a loud group of college guys. They slammed the drinks he made back and shouted hoarsely, raising their fists into the air.

A few minutes later, the bartender made his way up to a small stage with a karaoke machine and grabbed the microphone.

"This one's for you, Leah," he shouted. My name rumbled out over the noisy crowd. "Happy birthday!" Lifting the mike, he began to sing "I Guess That's Why They Call It the Blues," off-key, with his sexy accent rolling over the words. I couldn't wipe the grin off my face.

When the bar closed, the bartender took a cab home with me, across the bridge, his allure fading over the long ride as I sobered up. By the time we got to my apartment, I just wanted to get it over with. I watched from my mattress as he unlaced his shoes, took off his socks, unbuttoned his black shirt, and pulled off his black pants and white underwear. He put on a condom, lay over me, moving my clothing aside, and put himself inside me. I held on to his white shoulders and tried to push as close as I could into the nothingness.

• • •

A few months later, I woke in the middle of the night to the sound of shrieking laughter. Someone was banging on the door across from my apartment.

Shut the fuck up, I seethed, burying my head under the pillow. I had to be at work before eight to prepare for a presentation, which meant getting up at five forty-five. I needed sleep. Stuffing my fingers in my ears, I jealously contemplated my neighbors' seemingly easy lives.

I had chosen freedom, and I had paid the price: The loss of my family. Too much heartbreak. PID. But where was my delicious free-for-all? Where was all the candy sweetness of sin I had been so direly warned about? Wasn't that supposed to come along with its toxicity? All I seemed to encounter was rejection and disappointment. What other commandments would I have to break to access the goodies?

The shouting in the hallway continued all night. As light came through my window, I finally fell into a shallow sleep. It seemed only a moment had passed when my alarm went off, a sharp ringing beating into my brain.

I lay in bed, stiff with anger. I was exhausted, but my mind felt oddly clear. I saw everything with new eyes, as if I had wiped foggy glasses clean.

I took in my mattress on the floor. The dried paint running in frozen drips down the pockmarked walls. The wooden fish carving and the broken planter on the windowsill. The dollar-store necklaces hanging from a nail on the back of my door. The heap of dirty clothing on the floor.

I saw my life as if it were spread before me: the strict conventions of my professional job, the modest paycheck that denied me the flirty dresses I craved.

I thought of Tim, the long-haired hipster boy down the hall, who had introduced himself enthusiastically when I had first moved into the building. He had brought over a couple of beers, complimented my ass, and spent the night, but he had subsequently returned my enthusiastic greetings in the hall with grunts. And there had been Thomas, my old classmate, and the Irish bartender, and the one-night stand with a timid investment banker I had met through Craigslist, and Josh, the *Star Wars* fanatic I had met on the train, who had not been the boyfriend I'd thought he might become, and the hip-hop boys from Bushwick, and the biker boys from Park Slope, and the all too many disappointments I had pursued over the past year, as my liberated sexuality sent me hunting for satisfaction. Men flocked to me, but I was an abject failure at retaining their interest beyond a first or second date. It had been the same with Jacob and Nicholas and Duvi. Magic at first, that evaporated too soon.

My life was a mess, I realized, turning over and hiding my face under my arm. I was trying to create the life of a normal secular young person, but I was not normal. I would not metamorphose into a regular American girl. I was a crazy, broken slut, weighed down by a history that tormented me in nightmares. The life I was trying to craft was doomed to failure. I had to make a move, and there was only one direction in which to go.

I would become a prostitute.

The choice I made that morning felt inevitable. Girls who left Yeshivish life always became sluts and whores. This had been taught to me all of my life. I could never turn into a healthy irreligious woman. I now saw that this was not because of some divine punishment—no. It was because the journey out of the cloistered community I had been raised in was too difficult. The distance from modest girl to free woman could not be traversed. I would never have the confidence of a woman who'd received parental love regardless of her lifestyle choices. I would never relate to men the way a woman who had safely explored her sexuality in high school or college could. I would be stranded in black space between the world I came from and the world I wanted to enter, always falling short, always hurt, always failing. I might as well give up clawing away in the direction of a future that would never be mine. I might as well embrace my brokenness. I might as well wield it like a sword. I would not fall into the prophecy of doom; I would jump into it, feetfirst. I would be a smashing success at being bad.

Having rejected the laws of my upbringing, I had adopted few new morals. Sex was not sacred to me. And most importantly, I was good at it. My curves grabbed men's attention, their interest fueled my confidence, and in the act, my desperation to please left my lovers more than satisfied. I was clueless at relationships but fantastic at attracting eager men and thrilling them that first, magical time. I might as well pursue my strength, I figured. I did not pause over the dangers of prostitution. I did not worry about disease. The PID had probably left my insides dead. I felt I had nothing to lose.

At work, later that day, I opened up the websites for Craigslist and the *New York Times*. No one could see my computer screen without me knowing, but if someone did barge in, I had a quick decoy at hand.

"SWF seeks Mutually Beneficial Arrangement," I typed in the subject line. That was how the girls said it. I had seen the ads on desperate nights when my hunger had sent me browsing through the listings.

The cursor blinked as I peered into the mirror taped to my computer. Big brown eyes. Thick, long lashes. Broad, hooked nose. Tan skin.

"I'm petite," I wrote. "Pretty. Brown eyes, long brown hair."

How much money did a hooker make, I wondered. Probably a thousand dollars a night. Maybe two. No income tax. No Social Security. Two thousand bucks for a little flopping around. Two thousand dollars to be all sex. I could imagine myself in a tiny leather miniskirt, full breasts rising out of a glittery tank top, thick hair swirling over my shoulders as if an invisible fan whirled in front of my face. *Leah, man, she's a great lay. What do you do? I'm a prostitute.* I envisioned a new apartment, a penthouse in Manhattan: all white carpeting and silk sheets. Sleeping in till ten every morning, accepting wads of cash from men desperate for me. No more "Here's your reports." No more pin-striped trousers and button-down shirts and seven A.M. alarms. No more wrecked romances and depressing flings. No more frustration at being a failed good girl. I'd pursue the basest of base callings. I'd be the baddest bad girl around. *They pay me to fuck 'em. Sex on a stick.*

I clicked SUBMIT.

In minutes, my in-box was crammed with e-mails. I opened the responses, flipping from Craigslist to the *New York Times* site whenever anybody passed in the hall.

Most of the men had attached photos of their erections. The pictures made my stomach turn. Dumb men. Did they think that's why I was interested? I wanted the desperation in their fingers, the proof of their want digging into my stomach. I wanted a role that I could be good at.

The longest e-mail got my attention:

"I am a lawyer," it read. "My name is Stanley. I am 48 years young. I live on the Upper East Side. I have two adorable dogs named Lucy and Spot. I enjoy reading all kinds of mystery novels and going to the Met. I love the idea of a girl wanting a no-strings-attached relationship. So refreshing! Send me an e-mail and let's get to know each other!"

The guy's picture was a close-up of his face. He had heavy eyebrows that reached for each other across the bridge of his nose. His lined forehead merged into a bald head.

"Well, not no strings at all," I wrote. "I am doing this to make money." I cringed as I typed, afraid I'd sound greedy. Afraid I'd scare him off.

"That's no problem at all," Stanley replied, almost instantly. "You'll meet my needs and I'll give you what you need. I make a good living. I have no problem with that arrangement. Call me!" He included his number.

I could imagine giving him what he needed. How those eyes in the photograph would widen at the sight of me undressing. I could delight this Upper East Side lawyer. I could open my legs and leave him gasping. I'd had my share of gangster players and cool, hard hipsters. A forty-eight-year-old lawyer with two adorable dogs? Piece of cake. *I'll give you what you need.* I could see myself modeling lacy lingerie for him, leaving Saks loaded down with frothy bags, Stanley gushing at my elbow, hailing me a cab, massaging my feet, moaning as I pushed him back onto a new leather sofa.

I found a quarter in my desk and went out to the pay phone in the hallway.

"Hi," I said when he picked up. "Hi, it's Leah, the girl from the Craigslist ad." I cupped my hand around the receiver. There was no one in the hall, but you couldn't be too careful.

"Oh, hello there, Leah. It's great to hear from you." His voice surprised me. It was deep. Velvety. I'd thought it would be more high-pitched.

"Have you ever done this before?" he asked.

"No," I said with a nervous laugh. "Never."

"What are you? Hispanic?"

"No," I said. "I'm Jewish." It felt odd to wrap my mouth around the word "Jewish." It hardly seemed true anymore. I hadn't spoke to my parents in over a year, but they'd stopped considering me really Jewish a long time ago. My three older sisters, who pretended I was dead, and my six younger brothers and sisters, who barely knew I lived, felt the same. Jewish was in the blood, passed down through the mother, but it seemed that a girl could do enough things to wash that legacy away.

"What are you wearing?"

I described my skirt and turtleneck.

"Are you wearing underwear?"

I knew what he wanted to hear. "No," I lied.

"Mmmm. I would love to see you," he whispered. "I'm getting hard just imagining you, your skin, touching you. I'm touching myself, thinking about it. Can I see you? Can I come now? I'll hop in a cab. Can you see me?"

I loved the urgency in his voice. "Okay, fine." I gave him my address. It did not cross my mind that relaying this information to a stranger might be unsafe. Having rejected my conditioned fear of the stranger, I had never reintroduced the concept of prudent caution.

"Can't wait to see you in person," he said.

We said good-bye. I sent my boss an e-mail saying I had a headache and was going home.

My apartment was a mess, as always. I tugged the sheet over the mattress, scooped books off the floor, folded the bathroom towel, and hid a box of tampons behind the toilet. I grabbed a handful of Band-Aids and stuck them over the patch of crusty scars on my arm.

The doorbell rang, and I went to open the door. There he was. Stanley, wearing a leather jacket over a gray T-shirt, his hands shoved into the pockets of his jeans. He was shorter than I'd expected.

"Hey there," he said.

I stepped back, and he followed me inside. Stanley, I reminded myself as I gave my cheeks a quick pinch, pinking them up. What does a prostitute say? *Hey there—hello.* How does a woman sound sexy, mysterious, alluring?

Within seconds of entering my apartment, he stepped up to me, wrapped his arms around my shoulders, and buried his nose in my neck.

"Oh God," he whispered, pushing his body against mine. His fingers sank into my back and dragged down my body to my behind.

"Ohhh," he sighed. He fumbled at his waist, watching me as he pulled down his pants, lifted his shirt. I kept my eyes on my own body, yanking off my top and unhooking my bra quickly, so he wouldn't see the safety pin on the strap. I didn't want to have to look at him. Up close, it would be fine, but a few feet away, I found men doughy and misshapen. The sight of him would dry up whatever desire I had.

Think of the money, I reminded myself. Think of the hundreds of dollars waiting for you at the end of these few minutes. Think of seeing the boss tomorrow morning and saying, *I quit*. Think of walking into any store you want, pocket bulging with cash. Think of those black thigh-high boots with the cuffed tops that you saw in Macy's the other day. Perfect with a pair of fishnets and a little black dress. Imagine that Leah: gorgeous, in charge of a glamorous, badass life.

Stanley followed me to the bed. I lay down and he climbed on top of me, grabbing my breasts.

"God, you're beautiful," he moaned. I kept my eyes squinty, so he was just a fuzzy blur, as I arched my pelvis into him. I wanted it to start so it would end, so I could get to that point where he'd pulse with relief, mission accomplished. Satisfied. Grateful.

He pushed against me. I separated my thighs.

"You're wearing a condom, right?" I murmured.

"Yeah, yeah," he gasped as he plunged into me. His jaw dropped, his eyelids closed as he moaned. He was probably lying, but he was already in. There'd be no point in stopping him now.

"You're so tight, so hot," he groaned, thrashing against me. I kissed his cheek, his chin. My mind went blank, as it often did at this point, as we got into the friction, the repetitive back-and-forth of the thing.

He shoved. He pulled. He moved in and out.

"Yeah, oh yeah," I moaned, encouraging him along.

"Yeah, oh yeah," he cried, sinking his face into my shoulder, filling my nose with his smell of clean skin and cologne.

It went on. The thrusting. The rubbing. This was not like other men, engorged with appreciation for me, coming desperately, uncontrollably, as I moaned for them, kissed them, ran my hands over their flesh. Stanley kept going.

I clenched with each push in, tensed with each draw out. My insides were raw and hurting.

"Oh yeah, babe, so good. Oh yeah."

My jaw was tight, my eyelids squeezed shut. One, two, three, four, I counted in my mind. Thirty-one. Thirty-two. Thirty-three.

HaShem, I cried out silently. I had not used that name in so long. *HaShem. HaShem.* But I did not think God would hear a prayer from a rabbi's daughter impaled beneath a sweaty stranger.

"Oh, oh, oh."

And then, with his face buried in my shoulder, he moved his wet lips against my skin.

"Tell me you love me," he murmured.

I craned my neck to lick his ear. It was just a thing he was saying. He wouldn't be serious. Love. None of this—the nudity, the intercourse—meant a thing. But love, that was sacred.

I moaned, changing the subject. Sixty-one. Sixty-two.

He lifted his head. I opened my eyes. Drops of perspiration sparkled on his nose. His eyes bored into me.

"Tell me you love me." His palm framed my head. His body stilled as he stared at me, his thighs pressing into mine.

I reached for his skin with my lips. I loved nobody. I gave that to no one now.

Stanley pushed my face down with a firm hand.

"Tell me you love me," he repeated. His fingers sank into my cheek.

I swallowed hard.

"I. Love. You." I managed a smile.

He lifted his chin with a sigh and shuddered. He sat up. I saw that there was no condom.

"I've got to get home," he said, putting on his clothes. "My dogs are going to miss me."

I rolled up to sit and hugged my legs in.

"Um—what about—the—the money?" My voice was barely a whisper.

Stanley laughed. "Oh, don't worry," he said. "As long as you aren't asking for a black American Express card, I'm sure we'll work it out. I'll be in touch soon. Okay then."

He grabbed his jacket and waved good-bye.

The click of the door rang out in the quiet apartment.

I fell back on the sheets, rolling to face the wall, cupping my burning crotch in my hand, applying pressure to the chafed skin.

"Poor stupid little baby," I whispered.

"Are you feeling better?" my boss asked, stopping by my desk the next morning. I looked at him blankly. Only after he left did I remember my excuse of the day before.

Stanley's e-mail arrived at noon:

"Come to my place Saturday night, nine-thirty?"

I closed my Internet browser and busied myself with the papers that had accumulated on my desk. It was Friday. I had meeting after meeting scheduled and two major reports due. Would I go, I wondered, as I typed and spoke and smiled. Would I go see Stanley again?

At five o'clock, I stood in front of my tidied desk, purse in hand, e-mail open.

You're already halfway in, I thought. What was the point of

yesterday if you don't go through with it? You gotta be what this man wants; then he'll give you the money you need to quit your job, to establish yourself as a prostitute, to live a tough, cool life. It's got to be a nice amount—he's gotta pony up a nice chunk of cash for two times. And it's only sex, remember? What's a little more sex?

"Okay," I wrote him. "I'll come."

A reply popped up, almost instantly.

"Great! I'll wait for you in bed—just come into my apartment and find me there. Come inside to the room at the end of the hallway, undress, and come into bed with me. It will be like a fantasy! You are so sexy!"

Saturday night. I showered and shaved my legs, dressed in a pleather miniskirt and a silky silver blouse, and applied a fresh layer of Band-Aids to the scars on my arm. I leaned against the sink to peer into the cloudy mirror as I ran eyeliner around my eyes, using my fingertips to rub streaks of purple eye shadow on my eyelids.

"Hey! Come here, sexy mama," a man shouted from the bodega under the train tracks. Filled with a confusing mix of shame and power, I kept my face frozen as if I hadn't heard him.

On the train, I sat in the corner. I kept my eyes on three short hairs that sprouted on my left knee. A spot missed shaving. I tugged at the hairs, trying to pull them from the skin, but they were too short and slippery.

When I got to Stanley's building, I looked straight ahead, heels clicking across the marble lobby. The doorman didn't stop me. I took the elevator up and found the door to Stanley's apartment unlocked. I stepped inside.

It was dark. An amber pool of light came from a lamp on a small table. Two Chihuahuas bounded up and sniffed my ankles. I crouched down to pet them, scratching behind their ears, rubbing their tan coats. They jumped under my hands, trying to get more.

As a child, I had been terrified of dogs. Most Yeshivish Jews were. Vicious peasant dogs let loose in a hundred pogroms and images of watchful Nazi canines herding Jews persisted in our collective memory. In my early teens, I had gotten over my fear only because I worried that I was dishonoring God, fearing something so much, when only the Holy One should be able to generate that much terror. Now, a million years later, a million miles away, one of Stanley's dogs leapt at me and stuck his wet nose into my face, flicking his tongue to lick me. I gave him one more pat, then pushed him away. Stood up. The open door at the end of the hall waited.

The room was dark. It seemed large, and I could make out the shape of a bed in the middle. The sound of Stanley's heavy breathing filled my ears as I unbuttoned my blouse and unhooked my bra. Stanley's warm arms enveloped me when I slipped under the covers. His breath was hot on my face.

"God," he moaned, rolling on top of me. He was naked. His skin smelled of soap.

He covered my face with his hands, drawing his fingers over my neck and across my shoulders. He planted a few kisses on my cheek, his lips smooth and dry. His hard-on pressed against my thigh. Flicking his tongue into my mouth, he pushed into me. My body was not yet ready. My insides burned.

It's just sex, I thought. It's just sex. It's just sex. It's just sex.

It was like acting. I took pride in playing my role well. I could fool myself as well as him. My body began to respond, the burn fading as I got caught up in kissing him, touching him, sliding into the smooth gymnastics of sex. But I was relieved when, as I was resting on my elbows, butt in the air, trying to turn shudders into gasps of pleasure, he climaxed with a violent shiver.

Thank God, I thought, collapsing beside him. It's all over now. Good job, babe. Now sleep, morning, money, reinvention.

His slow exhalations faded as my exhaustion pulled me under.

Then his hand was on my stomach. His body over mine. His mouth at my mouth.

Fucking shit, I thought. Again? I swallowed hard to clean my sleepy mouth and opened to his kiss. One more time—I guess I can manage one more time. Think of the cash. Think of how sexy he must find you. Think of the stacks of cash waiting for you to fund any happy life you want.

I clutched Stanley's back, wincing as he pushed and grabbed at me. The pain seared up inside my body. My jaw fell back. I breathed in hard and pulled a rising yelp back to a whimper, hoping it sounded like pleasure. Stanley, his name is Stanley. You can tell him you're tired, tell him you want to stop. But I couldn't. I didn't. I kept on moving my body under his, praying for it to end. His body pumped like a piston, repeating the same motion endlessly.

"I love you," I told him when he asked me, over and over again. "I love you."

I couldn't stop the tears spilling down my cheeks. We rolled around the bed, the covers long ago kicked to the floor. Between his grunts, traffic rumbled on the street below. It was still dark, although it seemed as if it had been dark forever and morning must come soon.

When he finished with me, I curled into a ball on the other side of the bed, ten fingers pressing down the pain, shoulders shaking with quiet sobs that I tried to swallow down. Hookers don't cry, I thought. Pull it together. Get some sleep. Morning will be here any minute, and it will all be over. You will leave and never see this creep again.

His hand brushed my spine. Gently, he pulled me around to lie beside him. He slid on top of me. I bit the insides of my cheeks to keep from crying out as he entered me. Stop, stop, stop, stop, I pleaded silently. He kept on going. It felt as if my innards were being tattered on a cheese shredder. "I love you,"

I offered, desperately, before he even asked. "I adore you. You're the love of my life."

He finished. I buried my face in my elbow, my body vibrating with pain.

Stupid fucking bitch, stupid stupid bitch. Exhaustion washed over my anger. I lay on my stomach, limp as a rag doll. Darkness pulled me into its embrace. Oblivion.

A hand cupped my hip. A body behind mine. A hard dick against my butt. Fingers parted my sore legs, flipping me over.

When light crept into the bedroom around the curtains, it illuminated his frantic face above me. I tried to force a smile onto my face. He stopped and pulled out of me. I took a ragged breath. The absence of the pain hurt almost as much as the pain itself.

"Come." He pulled at my wrist. I staggered to my feet. He led me to his living room. Slate-colored walls crowded glass end tables and towering floor lamps. A large television faced a black leather couch.

"Lie here," he said, pointing to the couch. Dizzy, I dropped against the cool cushions.

"No, over the arm," he instructed me.

I crawled to the end of the couch. Arched my back over the arm. I smiled because he could see me in the light. I tried again to summon up some sound that would suggest that I was enjoying myself as he completed the job, his little dogs jumping around his feet.

When he finished, I was too numb to be glad. I got dressed, pulling my top over my arms, stepping into my skirt, weary and hurting. Please just give me the money already, I begged in my head. Please, say something about the money. I didn't have the strength to ask for anything.

He had put on a white bathrobe. I watched, relieved, as he

found his wallet. He walked to the front door. I followed him, my insides burning so hot it was hard to walk straight.

"I don't know if this is going to work," he said, a hand on the doorknob. He smiled at me. "I don't know if this is what you want, this whole arrangement, so I'm going to give you this, and let's leave it at that. It's what's best." He opened the door, three twenty-dollar bills in his hand.

I stared at the bills, at his calm face, at the money.

"Uh, I thought it would—I mean—that's only—" I was too weary to string words together.

"Here," Stanley said, handing me the cash. "I've got to go rest—it's been a long night, hasn't it? You should leave now."

I had no voice. No will. No thoughts. I took the money and left.

On the street, the sun poured between the city buildings. A blonde woman being pulled along by her two Great Danes looked me up and down. I shrank against the building to allow her and her dogs to pass, tugging at my skirt, pushing back my matted hair. The acrid stench of sex radiated from my body.

When I got home to my apartment in Brooklyn, my crusty razor was waiting for me. I sat on the stained toilet, put my feet up on the tub, and hacked at my skin until my arm was covered in a sleeve of blood.

After that night, the days passed in a blur. I arrived at work five minutes early, as I always had. I did my job with a smile, as I always did. I held everything in until five o'clock. Then I fell apart. At home, I lay on my bare mattress with the lights on, listening to pounding hip-hop blare through a small radio held close to my head, until four in the morning. I sat in my small bathroom and chopped at my skin with a razor until my arm was painted in blood. My beige refrigerator stood empty as my diet shifted to a consistent menu of Chinese takeout and candy.

I was three semesters away from graduating with a bachelor's degree and a nearly perfect GPA, but I couldn't walk back onto campus. I left a bundle of papers half finished and half a dozen e-mails from professors unanswered. I couldn't pretend that I believed in my ability to engineer my own life successfully. I had become a living embodiment of all of those cautionary tales I had been told, how leaving Yeshivish life ensured a miserable existence. I could never escape this bleak prophecy.

Eventually, the roaring anguish quieted. Left with an unending numbness, I passed the time in front of the television. I drowned my sadness with rows of sandwich crème cookies and jumbo bags of licorice. I avoided the sunshine, evaded summer, then slipped into the gray of autumn, welcoming the cold.

chapter fifteen

THROUGHOUT THE WINTER, my depression lingered. One evening, fed up by the unending cheer of Christmas carols played in the supermarket, I stomped home through the December slush, threw down my coat and groceries at the door, and headed to the bathroom. I grabbed my razor from a shelf of lipsticks and orphaned earrings. Cutting had become a regular ritual, like an evening prayer, a release from the day. I eyed my arm, seeking unbroken skin for the bite. My gaze drifted south, over the crusty railroad of scars, to the smooth expanse of my lower arm.

Go for it, a voice in my head whispered. *Why not?* My emotions felt so flat it seemed like nothing to watch my hand bring the razor down into my wrist, to watch the blade glint like a bracelet on my hand. I pressed the sharp edge into my skin, releasing a drop of blood.

Like a reverse Sleeping Beauty, I was snapped awake by the red bloom. I sprang up from my seat on the closed toilet and hurled the razor into the tub. I grabbed a dirty towel and pressed it to the small cut, falling over the sink, panting as I tried to catch my breath. This is your wrist, I thought with sudden lucidity. Leahchke, this is your blood.

I pulled the towel back from my skin. The small cut was

bare, the blood wiped clean. I sat back on the toilet and cradled my head in my arms.

Two weeks later, I held out my arm and a tattoo artist broke into the shallow scar I had made on my wrist, moving across my skin. I sucked my breath through clenched teeth as the high-pitched whine of the needle filled my ears.

My skin, I thought as the tattoo artist finished, dropping his ink. This is my goddamn flesh. You hear me, Leah?

We are neither all angel nor all animal, Rabbi Aziz, my seminary teacher, had explained years before. He had diagrammed the *aleph*, the letter that was now inked in blue-black perfection on my inner wrist. We must be a balance of the two.

Balance. Rabbi Aziz had also once said, "Maimonides says that when you're trying to adopt a trait, you must take it beyond your goal." He had held up a knobby finger to demonstrate. Bent it downward. "If you have a piece of grass that bends down and you want it to stand straight, you can't just push it up. You must push it all the way to the opposite side, and only then will it stand perfectly in the middle."

The cut on my wrist had been my wake-up call. I didn't want to end up back in a psychiatric hospital. I didn't want to die. I was done adhering to the prophecy that insisted that, having left my faith, I must lose my happiness.

The fresh tattoo, covered in Saran Wrap, was my action in the opposite direction. It stamped my soiled, scarred body as my own. It didn't belong to Stanley, or any man before him. It belonged to me. I had marked it with my mark. And my mark was an *aleph*. Jewish law forbade permanent markings on the skin, but I would get a Jewish tattoo. I would stop denying the complexity of my journey. I would remake the pieces of my life to form my own creation. They belonged to me, those fractured pieces. Nobody else.

When I got home from the tattoo parlor, I tossed my bloody razors in the garbage. I never cut myself again.

One night, as the wound was still healing on my raw skin, I had a dream.

My dream life had always been vivid. One of my earliest memories was of a dream from when I was four or five. I was riding a red tricycle up and down Beacon Street. "I'm going to flush you down the toilet if you ride past here one more time," the neighbor up the block bellowed. And indeed, there was a toilet sprouting in his yard like an overgrown white tulip. I couldn't resist my desire. I pedaled by again. The man grabbed me and flushed me headfirst down the toilet bowl.

I knew my dreams like an Eskimo knows snow: the roller coasters fueled by slices of pizza before bed, the visions that took me deep into the darkness, allowing me to carry up some nugget of truth when I woke, the frantic couplings with phantom men that left me shuddering in a release their human counterparts never offered.

The dream I had then, as my tattoo healed, was a rare kind. A single scene. Vivid but still. It came at the end of a long day at work and after a long evening with a good book. I had snuggled into the mattress's soft body, twisting in a frozen runner's stance. One leg up, one leg down, both bent against the bed, one arm below the pillow. Sleep crept up. My mind loosened. I was under.

Gandhi appeared. I recognized him from my high school history books. Round glasses, lined face. His bald head, beaked nose, and prominent ears were lit with a subtle strength. He seemed shy.

"You should have children," he said gently. The inflection of his voice made it both a compliment—he thought I would make a good mother—and a promise. Despite what the PID might have done to my insides, Gandhi seemed to be saying, he was close to the powers of the universe, and he'd make sure they did right by me.

When I awoke, I remembered every detail as brightly as if it had been a real conversation. I'm going to have children, I thought. I believed Gandhi entirely. Perhaps I no longer felt that I needed to be punished. Perhaps Gandhi was giving me permission to forgive myself.

After that night, I stopped worrying about my possible infertility. Gandhi's promise gave me faith.

It had been half a year since I had been a student at Brooklyn College. I wanted to go back. Determined to fix my mistakes and enroll in the upcoming spring semester, I reached out to my professors from the classes I had abandoned after the experience with Stanley, telling them I had been unwell. Most of them were surprisingly understanding, giving me assignments, which I quickly finished, and then adjusting my grades. There was only one grade I could not repair, a literature elective. The professor had moved away, and she said she could not help me.

I made an appointment with Dr. Harold Blau, the chair of the English Department. Dr. Blau was a tall man with a gray ponytail and a still gaze. His desk was piled high with messy stacks of papers that threatened to topple over. That seemed at odds with the careful arrangement of the books on the shelves and the formal art on the wall behind him.

"I dropped out in the middle of the semester last spring," I said, trying to explain my predicament. "I was——" My voice left me as I thought back to the rising depression that had swamped me after Stanley. "I was——in a rough spot," I finally said. I stroked my fresh tattoo. "I've reached out to my professors and passed all my other classes, but I got an F in Eighteenth-Century Literature, and the professor, Professor Clark——you know, she moved to Australia. My GPA was a 3.9 before that, and I really wish there was something I could do to fix that, so the F doesn't kill my whole GPA, and the professor said you might be able to help." I always lost my voice when I felt shy. I had to drag it over my tongue, pull the words out to try to explain to this distinguished man why I needed his help. Why he should care.

Since the encounter with Stanley, I had favored saggy jeans and cheap children's T-shirts. Together with my ragged short hair, they robbed my fine facial bones and thickly lashed eyes of their prettiness and disguised my large breasts, turning me into an invisible brown boy. But that night I'd worn stiletto-heeled boots and a wraparound dress, in an attempt to feminize my appearance and appeal to Dr. Blau.

"There are some options," Dr. Blau said, his hands resting on his muscular thighs, which strained against his pressed khaki pants. "But it depends on the circumstances. Why did you drop out?"

"I—I was having a—hard time." I flicked tears off my cheeks, trying to suck back the snot.

I had no defenses before a concerned adult. Gently, Dr. Blau pulled the story of Stanley from me with his careful questions, one detail at a time.

When his next appointment knocked on the door, Dr. Blau—or Harold, as he asked me to call him—invited me to see him again at the end of the week.

During our next conversation, his calm, attentive gaze drew out more stories, back to my parents' rejection of me and through much of the brokenness that had happened since. When it was time to leave, Harold walked me to the door. He paused before opening it.

"I don't normally—I don't ever—I don't do this," he said. "But I'd like to give you a hug."

His arms came around my back. My head nestled halfway up the broad chest of this tall, powerful, gentle goy. His stiff shirt pressed against my cheek. He smelled of baby powder with a tinge of the sharp odor of an older person. I could have stayed in that embrace for an eternity.

• • •

There were forty-two years between Harold and me. He had been the chair of the English Department for nine years and was married with four grown children, now in their late twenties and early thirties. I knew that the world would judge our difference in age, but I didn't think it was creepy. He was exactly what I needed. I gave him a taste of youth and uncomplicated adoration, and he offered me support and guidance and love, quickly becoming a surrogate, if somewhat incestuous, parent.

Pupa, I eventually called him, an obvious derivative of "Papa." Evening after evening, we sat side by side in chairs in his office, talking about my life.

"What do you want from your future?" he would ask.

"I want to get married and have children," I would tell him every time. I wished I had faith in my career ambitions, but I felt, having never been encouraged, that it would be impossible for me to have that much belief in myself, to aim that high. Instead, I clung to a future with motherhood at its center. Especially now that, with Gandhi's promise, I believed that I could have kids.

The long hugs I shared with Harold soon led to kisses, then snuggles. One night we finally attempted to have sex, on his office floor. But when I saw Harold hovering above me, I was overcome with a rush of fear, as if I was sullying some sacred bond. He drew back in horror.

"That look. Oh, that look." He gathered me in his arms, pressing his cool lips to my forehead, his erection forgotten. His love overpowering his desire was a soothing balm for all the painful sexual relationships of my past.

Eventually, we did get to fitting our bodies together in that practiced way, but most of the time we avoided it. I lay in his lap for hours as he stroked my limbs with his fingertips. The only thing like it were the razors I had used in the past to open my skin to help me breathe. Harold's touch drew no blood, but it gave me release.

Sensuality without intercourse was new to me. The meandering gentleness of our play made me feel free to experience my sexuality without shame. Harold's adoration saturated me with confidence and calm.

His influence was also pragmatic. "You realize that if you respond to that, it's an invitation for him to continue?" he said when I showed him a flirtatious e-mail from a colleague. "Guys are always fishing. If you don't protest, he'll charge forward."

I had never realized that secular men and women played a clear game with rules. I had walked into their world as a naïve teenager fresh from a gender-segregated society, and it had closed over my head before I could catch my breath. With Harold's commentary, I began to understand how my actions were being interpreted and what others meant by theirs, learning about sexuality in a way that made me feel less like a defenseless victim.

The change in me, as our relationship blossomed, was not only sexual. With Harold's support, I began to voice my opinions on politics, culture, the world. I had always shut down when talking to men, believing I just had to smile and agree with whatever they said. Harold encouraged me to break out of that shell. He helped my voice grow strong.

Mostly Harold and I saw each other in his office, but when an elaborate lie would allow for it, he visited my apartment. One spring evening he came home with me after my classes ended. On the train, we acted the professor and student. When we got off and the sky exploded with hard needles of rain striking against our backs, we ran hand in hand for my apartment, breathless with laughter. Inside, we yanked off our soggy shoes, spraying puddles of water on the floor. The phone rang.

"Hi, Leah? It's Deena."

My younger sister. We hadn't spoken in a long time. I got news in snippets from Elisha, who I still spoke to occasionally, although our relationship had weakened as his family had grown. He had told me that Deena was engaged. At twenty-one, she was embarrassingly old. Her irreligious sister had probably affected her marital options.

"Is everything okay?"

Harold took off his soaked jacket and put it over the chair. He helped me out of my jacket, one arm at a time, as I shifted the phone from hand to hand.

"My wedding is in eight and a half weeks, *im yertze HaShem*. I'd like you to come," Deena said. "It would be nice if the whole family could be there together."

"I don't think it's a smart idea," I said, lifting the phone from my face as Harold pulled my shirt over my head. Caught off guard by my sister's friendly invitation, I automatically slipped into a matching tone, as if we had no history, as if we were normal siblings. But still, Pittsburgh seemed like a distant mirage. I couldn't imagine trying to fit the woman I now was back into that place.

"It'll be fine. Please, Leah, you should come."

"I can't, Deena," I said. "It's too much pressure."

"Well, this weekend we're having a *vort* in Pittsburgh, *im yertze HaShem*, to share our *simcha* with Tatte's congregants. Would you come out to Pittsburgh for Shabbos?"

I considered her invitation. I couldn't deny that I still had the ache of homesickness buried somewhere in my chest. It had been a long time.

"If Mamme and Tatte say it's okay, I'll come."

We said good-bye. I let my legs go and fell into Harold, sinking slowly enough for him to catch me.

"I don't want sex," I said, pulling away from his fingers, his mouth.

"Who was that?" he asked, wiping my wet bangs off my forehead.

"My sister. Deena."

"What did she want?"

"I don't want to talk about it." Tears welled in my eyes. It had been years since I had spoken with my sister. Her sudden friendliness was more upsetting than the usual silence. It reminded me of all the sisterhood I had missed out on, all the intimacy of family I had lost. "Please, Pupa, make me feel better."

Harold curled his large body around mine and ran his palm over my arm. I pushed into him until all of me was held securely by him, like a mollusk in a shell.

Later that night, after Harold left, Deena called back. Our parents had suggested, she told me, that I come to a dinner planned only for the family on Sunday, rather than joining the community for an entire weekend of celebrations.

It was just as well, I thought. That would be more manageable. I agreed to be there.

When I woke on Sunday morning, it was still dark out. I braided my hair and dressed in a skirt and a sweater that were modest enough for my family and comfortable enough for the long ride to Pittsburgh. I found a couple of Band-Aids and slapped two on my wrist, hiding my tattoo. The bus to Pittsburgh left Penn Station at five. The sun stained the sky bubblegum pink as the bus rumbled out of the city.

Deena picked me up from the bus station in Pittsburgh, filling the silence in the car with details about the cutlery set she was choosing for her new home and the floral arrangements for her wedding. I nodded and laughed along, but I was barely listening.

A tree-lined avenue reminded me of a walk I had taken there with my father, when I was young. My mother had called him to punish me when her slaps and threats were not enough to silence a tantrum. I had trotted after my father as we walked in silence.

"Leahchke," he had finally said, after a long stretch of quiet. "You're such a good girl—please be more respectful to your mother."

How I had cherished his attention!

The giant rambling home I remembered now looked small.

The grass in the yard rose in waves. One of the trees that had guarded the front door had been cut to a low stump.

Deena stopped me on the sidewalk.

"Listen," she said, folding her slim arms across her chest. "I just want to tell you—" She paused, hesitating. "Um. Mamme asked if, maybe, it would be best if you didn't touch any of the kids."

"What?"

"She's afraid, *chas v'shalom*, that you'll give them some disease." Deena avoided my eyes. "Because you have relationships with men. Also, she asked if it's possible for you not to eat off the regular dishes. You don't mind using paper plates, right? Because she's worried about disease."

"Why did you even invite me?" I spat out.

My little sister shrank back at my anger.

"My fiancé thought it would be better if we didn't ignore you," she murmured. "That's what his rabbi believes." She turned toward the house.

I wasn't ready to let it go. "What did I ever do to be treated this way?" I demanded.

Deena stopped and raised her arched eyebrows as if the answer was obvious.

"I'll have you know that Mordy is struggling in yeshiva," she said. "Mamme and Tatte are having a very hard time with him. He used to be a very good boy. They are devastated."

"Mordy? What are you talking about? I haven't seen him in years. What does that have to do with me?"

"You don't remember? When you bought him that gift for his birthday? What did you think that was going to do? Everything has consequences. Of course he's having problems now."

It took me a moment to understand, but there was only one birthday gift I had ever given Mordy that she could be referring to: that yeshiva-regulation white button-down shirt I had bought him years before. Did they really see me as so toxic, I wondered, that even a gift, coming from me, could be poison?

"He's in yeshiva," Deena said. "He didn't come home. But stay away from the others." Brushing her shiny hair off her face, she turned and stepped through the front door.

I took a deep breath, pulled at my collar to make sure it was high enough, and followed my sister inside.

"Hello," my mother called as she rushed around the kitchen, preparing dinner. She seemed aged and dried out. Her wig was chopped above the shoulder and shaped roughly, without style. Her shirt and skirt were both black.

The number of babies in the house shocked me. There were eight, at least, between my older sisters. I was struck with a stab of jealousy as I watched my sisters wrap their arms around their cherubic toddlers. I wished, for one fierce moment, that I could exchange my life, with all of the joy of secular freedom and Harold's love, for the motherhood my sisters enjoyed.

The front door opened. My father entered with my brothers-in-law, a black parade that mobilized its audience to straighten their wigs and smooth their skirts. My father's shirt no longer ballooned over his stomach. It tucked straight into his belt, as if he had deflated with age. He nodded hello at me, but I was too unnerved to respond. By the time I pulled myself together enough to smile and nod back, he had turned away.

"Dinner's ready," my mother called. A line formed at the kitchen sink. When it was my turn, I poured the water over each hand twice with the silver cup, drenching my skin from wrist to fingertips, the blessing coming back to me as I dried my fingers on a damp towel. It gave me a strange feeling, doing this thing I used to do daily after such a long time of not doing it. Homesickness washed over me, even as I stood in my former home. It wasn't this I had missed: the cracked linoleum floor, the boxy rooms, the photographs of rabbis on the walls, the piles of LEGOS underfoot. It was myself. Homesickness was the ache for the girl I used to be, that sexless, fuzzy-haired child, so blindly confident that she would have an easy life, always protected by a vigilant God.

In honor of Deena's engagement, we ate at the Shabbos table, which had been set with Shabbos china and platters of roast chicken and freshly tossed salad and crispy potato kugel and challah still hot from the oven. I looked around, unsure of where to sit.

"Here, Leah, here," my mother said, beckoning. She gestured to a chair between Deena and my older sister Shaindy. The place was set with a paper plate and a white plastic fork, knife, and spoon. I squeezed into my seat and helped myself to a chicken thigh. I ate silently, my mouth flooding with joy at my mother's cooking. The familiar citrusy flavor of the chicken and the soft give of the warm bread on my tongue were more delicious than any of the cheeseburgers or nonkosher candy bars I now regularly ate.

I watched the animated faces around the table, listening to the lively conversations flowing over and around me. The family had changed during the time I had been gone. Now it seemed accepted that the men sat near my father and talked about learning while the women sat at the other end, gossiping about babies and cooking. When I was young, we sat around the table and shared one conversation. My father would look to my adoring eyes when he wanted to start a story.

"Do you know the tale of the fisherman and the Shabbos angel, Leahchke?" he would ask. Everyone would fall silent. I would shake my head no, glowing with joy at having the question directed at me.

Now one of my nephews sat on my father's lap. He kept one arm around his grandson's belly, affectionate and possessive in a way I had never seen him act with his own children.

"The *issur* of tefillin on Shabbos is not *d'orysa mamash*," my father was saying to one of my brothers-in-law, while at the other end of the table my older sister Shaindy asked Deena, "Did you see the newest Carly?"

"Oh my, yes," Deena said. "It's unreal how much it doesn't look like a wig. I have never seen another wig like it. Did you think about getting one?"

"There's a *gezeira shava* on that in Bava Kama," one of my brothers said to my father. My father nodded. "Of course. *Tachas-tachas*. But there's a *kabbalah* on that. For a *kal vachomer*, you don't need a *kabbalah*."

"I styled a Carly, for a friend," Shaindy said to Deena. "It is gorgeous, much more natural than the Gigi. I'm thinking about it."

I felt like an anthropologist, studying this tribe of people who, with their watchful eyes, dark skin, and small bones, re-sembled me yet were now as alien to me as a family of foreign-ers, their religiosity and gender divisions even more extreme than those of my distant childhood. My romanticized impression of my youth evaporated as I observed them. Neither conversation was uplifting to me. Neither seemed profound.

When I finished eating, I sat with my arms folded and lis-tened, waiting for it to be over. Finally, the dessert plates were cleared away. The men recited Grace After Meals aloud while the women whispered along.

Deena offered to drive me back to the bus station. I found my mother at the kitchen sink, elbow-deep in dishwater.

"I'm leaving now," I said.

My mother raised her shoulder to push back a strand of wig hair stuck to her face.

"Good-bye, Leah," she said, with more softness in her voice then I'd expected. "I would walk you out, but this—" She nodded at the water. "You understand? Be well."

"Good-bye." I wished I could take her gentleness as an invi-tation to say more, but I was afraid to ruin the moment. My fa-ther was coming down the stairs as I walked to the front door.

"I'm leaving now, Tatte." I wanted to give him one last chance to say something. To see me. To belatedly rescue me.

"Safe journey," he said and made to turn down the hallway.

"I miss you. I miss you, Tatte." The words ripped out of me. I couldn't stop them.

He turned. He didn't say anything. He just looked at me. The floodgates opened. The words came pouring out with the tears.

"What did I do? Why have you abandoned me? What happened? Why must you be like this to me? What kind of father are you that you could just leave me for all these years? I needed you! How could you be so cold and indifferent to me? Why did you treat me like I was garbage, like you walked away and never looked back, never cared enough to see if I was okay, never thought maybe I needed you, maybe I needed a father even if I wasn't the perfect daughter? How could you just decide not to be there for me anymore?"

My father stood still, his hands clasped behind his back. I waited, breath held, tears dripping off my chin.

"I am not interested in being attacked by you," he finally said.

I froze, tensing my jaw, my shoulders, my butt, holding tight.

"No one wants to face certain difficult realities," he continued, speaking in a modulated voice, as if he were giving a sermon. "One way you often cope with your difficult realities is by putting the blame on others and not taking responsibility yourself. I am not a therapist, but I have enough experience with addictions among my congregants to know that what you have sought from me is my approval to feed your habit. Codependency is the term, I believe. I refuse to do that for you, because I love you. I do the best I can. It may not be enough for you. But I suspect that nothing anyone does will ever be enough. The problem lies within yourself. So does the solution. It is counterproductive to pursue this subject further. Good-bye."

He walked away. I sobbed without restraint, hugging the white plaster hallway as if it were the Western Wall. It was too much. Why had I come? Why had I held on to my love for this place, for these people?

Outside, a horn beeped twice. Deena, waiting to drive me to the bus station. I wiped my eyes, cleaned my glasses on my skirt, and walked out into the cool late afternoon.

chapter sixteen

THE BUS DROVE THROUGH THE NIGHT, stopping in numerous cities along the way. When I finally arrived in New York I didn't have time to go back and forth to Brooklyn, so I slowly drank a large cup of coffee at a diner and then went to work, then class, and then, finally, at nine o'clock in the evening, to Harold.

"How was it?" he asked, closing his office door behind me.

"Ghastly," I sighed, relieved that I had someone to confide in.

"Poor baby." He stroked my bangs off my face with his knuckles. "Do you want to tell me about it?"

I shook my head.

"I just want you to make it better. Just make it better, Pupa."

He nodded, quiet for a moment. Then he directed me to a bare spot on the wall. He looked around for a minute, then turned back to me.

"Give me your socks."

I was surprised, but I liked his authoritative tone. I pulled down my knee-high socks and handed them to him, embarrassed that they didn't smell fresh. I tried to avoid laundry when I could. Harold removed my glasses. He took one sock and stretched it in front of my eyes, around my face, tying it behind my head.

"Okay?"

"Don't ask, just do." I wanted to be his inanimate object. Then I would have no pain, no memory. No responsibility.

The other sock pressed against my lips, a gag. I sighed. The tension slid off my shoulders. He undressed me without pausing to touch me. His breathing was quick with excitement. When I was naked, he stepped away. I heard him rustling at the far end of the room.

Then his hands were on my wrists, gently lifting them up over my head. A rope was tied around them, bringing my palms together. The rope pulled taut, affixed to something above me. Its rough surface dug against my back, curled around one thigh, up around my waist, biting into my belly and knotted around my breasts.

I waited. I sucked air in through my nostrils, the sock's odor tickling my nose. My skin strained for his touch. For long, agonizing moments there was nothing. Just rope. Just cool air. Then Harold's finger stroked my right instep, lightly tracing its curve, up and around my ankle. Goose bumps raced up my leg. My sadness dissipated. I felt alive. Electrified. Every sensory receptor on my skin was awake, from my arms stretched above my head to the soles of my bare feet.

I realized I needed to pee.

"Pppp," I said, through the sock gag around my mouth.

His hands were at my hair, untying the sock.

"What is it? Does it hurt? Are you okay, darling?"

"I need to pee. I'm so sorry, after you tied everything."

"Wait a minute. Just hold it in for a second."

I waited in the darkness, listening to papers shuffling and a clink of something I couldn't identify.

I heard him breathing as he approached. Then his hands were on my thighs. He put something cold and smooth between them. Something hard, like plastic or glass.

"You can pee now," he said. "Go ahead."

"What is that?" My ears and nose strained to pick up a clue.

"A vase."

"You seriously want me to pee into a vase?"

"Go ahead." He stroked my hip with a warm hand. "Let go."

Are you kidding, I thought. No way. My body won't. But after a moment of him standing there silently, patting my skin, I relaxed. Pee splashed into the glass. Embarrassed, I felt my shoulders come up, my lip catch in my teeth.

When I was done, he pulled the glass away. His hand came back between my legs. He wiped the last drops of urine from me with a tissue, as if I were his child. As if he were the parent I'd never had, gentle and adoring. His fatherly love seeped deep into my jagged heart.

"Take me down," I begged. He pulled the sock off my eyes, unwound the rope from a nail on the wall above me, and scooped me into his arms.

Midterms came and went in a flurry of late-night studying. Harold caught my feet in his hands as I lay sprawled across the couch in his office, nose-deep in a book on Mexican magic realism.

"Hey," I cried, twisting around. "I'm ticklish!"

"Ticklish? Really?" His fingers continued to drift over my curled sole, sending currents up my spine. I grabbed him. We wrestled, me giggling, him chuckling, my arm swiping my textbook and sending it flying to the floor with a thud.

I didn't do as well as I had before. Two A's, three B's. Loneliness had kept me focused on academic excellence. I had had nothing else. With Harold, my studying was always distracted, secondary.

"How did you do on your midterms?" Harold asked a few days after he'd handed in his grades for his students. "You haven't said anything."

I shrugged. I didn't want to admit to him that I wasn't a perfect student anymore. I was afraid he might be disappointed in me.

"You're not going to tell me?" he asked, coming around from his desk, where he had been checking his e-mail. I sat up on my heels on the chair and beckoned to him.

I tugged at his purple-and-pink-striped tie until his face was level with mine.

"I'm going to tell you," I whispered in his ear. "I'm going to tell you everything. First I'm going to unbuckle your belt, like this, see? And then, then, very slowly I'm going to unbutton this here and then . . ."

My voice faded, and my body took over the conversation. I loved playing the confident lover with him. His constant affection gave me the self-assurance I needed to make sex mine.

Harold kept pushing me to reimagine a better future.

"Are you ever going to tell me what you want to do once you get your degree?" he asked one evening. "You're talented and smart. You can do anything. You should start making a plan."

I shrugged. "Anything? Really, Pupa? I could never be someone like you."

"What do you mean?"

"You know. You're so—" I struggled for the right word. "Distinguished," I finally said.

"I wasn't born a professor, you know. Go to grad school and you can be at least as good an academic as I am."

"I can't even imagine that." Harold's expression was startlingly serious. Didn't he understand? "It's like asking a penguin to become a tiger. It's just not how I was raised."

"You're hardly the woman you were raised to be, Leah."

"But—I don't know. Graduate school?"

"Graduate school. What do you want to study? What kind of degree do you want to get? Where do you want to go?"

He was growing insistent for answers, as if I was expected to make a plan in that moment. For the first time, I considered his questions in earnest. I was at Brooklyn College because it was local. Because it had accepted me. But if I went to graduate school, I could go anywhere. I pictured myself on some sunny campus, younger students looking admiringly at me, just as I admired the graduate students I encountered. Maybe I could become someone accomplished. Maybe when people talked about me back home, they wouldn't just say, *Oh, Leah, the rabbi's daughter, the one who left home whose life fell apart.* They'd say, *Oh, Leah, the smart one. She went to college. And then she went on to graduate school.*

"So, grad school?" Harold asked.

I lifted my chin, drew in my breath, and paused for a long moment. "Harvard," I said finally.

"Harvard?" he asked.

"Harvard," I repeated, waiting for him to laugh. Graduate school was a ridiculous idea by itself, but Harvard—that was sheer craziness. Even as a Yeshivish child, I'd known of Harvard. I'd known that only the smartest people went there. Not a broken refugee from a sheltered world.

"Well, then," Harold said. "You have to think backward from Harvard and figure out what steps you need to take to get where you want to go."

I laughed. It was an unattainable fantasy. That evening, like all our evenings together, evolved into a half-naked snugglefest on his office floor. But his serious belief in my dreams stuck with me.

I had always been taught that people who left the Yeshivish community were failures. I had almost succumbed entirely to that stereotype. But if I could somehow, through some miracle, get into Harvard, then I could prove to the world that just because I wasn't Yeshivish and married with babies didn't mean I couldn't live a life worthy of respect.

Later that evening, I stopped into a Rite Aid and bought a poster board and a pack of felt markers. At home, sweating in the heat, I stripped to my boy-cut underwear and beige bra and kneeled on the floor in front of the poster board, marker poised.

What if I were actually in charge of my life, I thought. What if I could create the future of my choosing?

188 · LEAH VINCENT

I had a good job, but it wasn't fulfilling. I thought about the businesswomen who strode through the streets of Manhattan, chins up, on top of the world. I thought about Harold's office, how he would swivel in his chair, mail from academics in Chicago and London piled on the desk in front of him. I thought about my mother, sitting in the dark living room, a baby at her breast, toy building blocks scattered at her feet.

Uncapping one of the markers, I wrote on the poster board: *Affirmations: I am happy. I have a wonderful life. I will be accepted into Harvard. I will build a successful career doing—* Doing what? I wondered. What did I want to do? I rubbed my bleary eyes. It was getting late. *Something that I love,* I scrawled and then taped the poster to my wall.

In the morning, I stopped in front of the sign while pacing the room, brushing my teeth.

"I am happy," I garbled out loud, spitting toothpaste froth. "I have a wonderful life. I will be accepted into Harvard. I will build a successful career doing something that I love."

That night, before I went to sleep, I stood and recited the list again. It became a ritual, like the Shema I'd recited every morning and every night as a child.

I spent all Sunday at the Barnes & Noble in Union Square, reading study guides for the GRE, the standardized test for graduate school. Maybe I would go to graduate school. Maybe a miracle would occur and I would get into Harvard.

When September came, I signed up for a full load of evening and weekend classes, cramming them into my schedule so I could graduate at the end of the year.

One autumn evening, about ten months after I began seeing Harold, my phone rang. It was shortly after nine o'clock. I was lying in bed, playing an online GRE vocabulary game, dressed in cotton underwear and an old T-shirt that had long lost its collar and sleeves to a big-mouthed pair of scissors. A breeze swirled through the open windows of the apartment, ruffling the edges of the drawings I had taped to the walls.

"Hello?"

"Hi, darling." It was Harold, making his nightly call as he walked from the subway station to his apartment.

"Hey, Pupa."

"How are you doing?"

"Mmmm . . . okay. How was that meeting?"

"It was unbearable. It dragged on forever and ever. The professor—" His voice cut off.

"Pupa?"

"Hold on— Listen, I think she might be calling me. I'm going to go—I'll call you tomorrow, okay?"

She. The huge invisible *she* who I tried to pretend didn't exist.

"Okay," I sighed. "Love you lots."

"Love you, too."

I wasn't interested in the GRE anymore. I wished *she* would stop interfering with my life. I wished he would just leave her already. I felt no guilt over loving a man married to another woman. I wasn't the one who had recited any vows, I rationalized. Besides, Harold couldn't stand being with his wife. I didn't understand his hesitation over leaving her. When we talked about it, he'd say that we would never work. That I was too young to shackle my life to a man almost three times my age. But still, we fantasized about living together, having a child together, naming her Sage, imagining the light eyes the baby would get from him, the dark curls I would give her. Picturing a life where we could wake up beside each other every morning, my future secure in his heart.

I stood and faced my affirmation poster, raced through the statements, and fell back into bed to wait for sleep.

That night, I dreamed I was running down a dark alley in Jerusalem, trying to find my way to the Western Wall. Suddenly, two men accosted me. They said their friend had caught Harold. They had beaten him. My hands flew up to cover my eyes. The walls around me were flat and unyielding. One of the men rubbed his wet penis on my face. I punched him. I pushed and got free. Naked, I ran on air, over the domed roof of my father's synagogue. My mother raced behind me shouting, trying to catch my arm as I frantically pumped my legs to float higher and higher and away.

I woke in a sweat. The night was quiet. I turned and burrowed under my covers, trying to pull free of the dream.

In the morning I called Harold's cell phone. He didn't pick up. I called his office phone. There was no answer. I called both lines again, and again. There was no answer at either. Nauseous with worry, I scanned the news, looking for his name, terrified that he might have been mugged or in an accident.

After three days of silence, my phone rang at work.

"Hi."

My stomach sank. In his breath, in his voice, I could hear something awful.

"I've been so worried about you. Are you okay?"

"She found out. I can't talk. I need to deal with this. I'll call you later."

"But—okay—I love you. I love you so much. Do whatever you have to do."

"Okay, good-bye."

A wall had thundered down between our hearts. I could hear it in his voice.

When work ended, I didn't go to school. I went home and got into bed. "It isn't fair," I sobbed into my pillow. "It isn't fucking fair."

Harold didn't call.

For four days I couldn't eat. I had no room for food. My body was swollen with sorrow. I stumbled through my waking hours with bleary eyes, my heart a hard stone. On the fifth day, I stopped at a deli after work and bought a box of doughnuts. When I got home, I sank to the floor and tore open the package. I ate one doughnut after another: three chocolate, three powdered, three jelly, pressing down my emotion as I filled myself with food.

As I crammed the last of the ninth pastry into my mouth, vomit rose in my throat till I couldn't breathe. I put the box with the remaining three doughnuts in the garbage and stumbled to bed.

I hate you, I hate you, I hate you roared through my sugar-polluted blood. Who did I hate? Harold? His wife? Myself?

In the middle of the night I woke up starving, my stomach raging for food. I flipped on the light. Stumbling against the wall, blinking in the brightness, I pulled the crushed box of doughnuts out of the garbage can. The three remaining pastries were still soft. They collapsed in my mouth, one after another.

Then the phone rang. I jumped. Harold!

It was a woman.

"Leah?"

I hung up, my hand shaking. It was her. I knew it.

The phone rang again. And again. And again. I didn't want to take it off the hook, because I thought Harold might call me, but I didn't want to pick up the phone, because I was sure that if I did, it would not be Harold, it would be her. I could not form coherent thoughts. The phone rang all night, piercing my terror-filled sleep. The next evening, the phone rang from the moment I came home from work. Its clang hammered into my exhausted brain. Finally, I picked up the receiver.

"Do you know what you've done?" the woman screamed. "Do you know that you have destroyed my marriage? Have you no shame?"

The violence in her voice set my heart racing. I couldn't take it in. I was the little girl who was losing her lover. I was the one who had been harmed time and time again. I had no room for Harold's wife's pain in my heart.

"You are evil," she said. "A young girl seducing a married man. What you have done is pure evil. Do you understand me? Do you understand me? DO YOU UNDERSTAND ME?"

"I hear you," I said with great reserve. I didn't want to engage with her. I didn't want this woman to imagine that I accepted her view of the situation. Harold was the one who was married, not I. He had come to me, offering his love; I had not forced it from him. Our bond had been empowering, almost sanctified. I did not feel guilty about our relationship.

Harold's wife exploded.

"ARE YOU FUCKING KIDDING ME? You *hear* me? You *hear* me? You better hear me, you little slut, you fucking cunt! You are one sick little motherfucker! You just wait and see what's coming to you, you disgusting shit!"

There were muffled sounds in the background, screaming. Harold came on the line and said, "I love my wife. I have always loved my wife."

He sounded like a hostage. Like a broken old man. I abhorred Harold's wife for crushing him with her anger.

I replaced the phone receiver in its cradle with a trembling hand. Harold was gone. He had made his choice.

At work the next day, I sat on a closed toilet in a bathroom stall, sobbing into my elbow as coworkers flushed on either side of me. That evening, I trudged home to bed and lay there for hours. Unable to move, with my heart in pieces, I mourned for Harold as I had never mourned for my own father, in a great cleansing sorrow. Still awake at dawn, I watched the sun fill my room, its relentless shine creeping across the wooden floor.

chapter seventeen

MY RELATIONSHIP WITH HAROLD had been so therapeutic that I had refused to acknowledge that a love affair with a married senior citizen was unlikely to last forever. He was the father I had always wanted, and I could not entertain the idea that I would lose this parent, too. His abrupt abandonment of me induced vicious flashbacks to my own parents' abandonment. I had not expected Harold to be so heartless. I had not expected that his love could disappear in an instant.

But I was no longer a young, defenseless girl, and I was unwilling to blame myself for this failed relationship. In the days that followed our break, I wrote angry letters addressed to Harold, demanding to know how he could have misled me. How he could have turned off his love so swiftly. I did not send the letters, but expressing my anger outwardly instead of swallowing it down was a refreshing change.

I was sad, but I was also proud of myself. I did not return to cutting. I did not fall into a spiral of obliterating self-hatred. I could feel the iron in my core. I handled this devastation with a strength I had never before possessed.

Despite my new strength, I could not convince myself to reengage with the dreams of graduate school that Harold had helped me believe in. My loss was too fresh, too painful. I tried to stay in a state of neutral denial about my future, focusing only on my job, on the day-to-day.

Then I got an e-mail reminding me of my upcoming GRE test. No. Fuck no, I thought. There's no way I'm taking it. There's no point anymore. It was all a stupid pipe dream.

But I didn't delete the e-mail. It sat in my in-box, waiting.

One evening, sneezing into my hand while rushing to the bathroom, I stubbed my toe on my GRE math workbook. "Shit," I shrieked, hopping and scowling at the book. When I was done peeing, I skirted the book and made my way back to my mattress. I was numbing my heartache on the season finale of *America's Next Top Model* on YouTube, eating up the doe-eyed faces and the shallow drama. But now, during the final runway walk, moments before the winner was declared, I found I no longer cared which long-legged girl became America's next top model. In fact, I could no longer bear to watch another moment of flat stares and melodramatic stomping. I had only been on hiatus from my future. It was time to return from mourning. I paused the show. Closed the laptop. Reached for the math book.

From that night on, I resumed my study schedule. I pushed my sorrow to the back of my mind like a hard brick crammed into a sandwich bag, squeezing mathematical equations and archaic vocabulary words around it. I returned to my poster of affirmations and began reciting them again each night. Even with Harold gone, I could not unsee what he had helped me envision.

Test day arrived. I reached for my alarm before it went off. *What do you think?* I asked myself as I lay naked, sprawled across the mattress, contemplating my day. *Can you really do this?*

The test was a slab of wood bobbing in the ocean, just out of my reach. Being with Harold had gotten me this close; if I could grab it, I thought, hoist myself up and out of the depths, I could finally be saved.

I brushed my teeth, toothpaste foaming in my mouth, itchy tears veiling my eyes. I missed Harold. I need him, I thought, remembering the comfort of his love. I wish I could hear him say, *Good luck*. I wish I could have one last hug. Without his encouragement, I'm gonna freeze, I thought. I'm gonna fail.

I dressed and spoke my affirmations out loud into the quiet apartment: "I am happy. I have a wonderful life. I will be accepted into Harvard. I will build a successful career doing something that I love."

Enough's enough, I thought firmly as I caught the train downtown. Harold might have helped turn things around in my life, but the way he'd broken up with me was royally dickish. He was not my savior. This was my life. Enough throwing myself at Harold's memory or any other man, looking for redemption. I can do this on my own goddamn terms. Watch me.

And I did.

The exam had two sections, each scored on a scale of 800 points. I needed a 680 in each to be considered by Ivy League schools.

At the end of the exam, my score flashed on the screen:

710 on the quantitative section;

770 on the verbal section.

I pushed my seat back, adjusted my glasses, blinked hard. The numbers stood firm. I looked at the frozen heads fixed to computers on either side of me. *Look what I've done*, I wanted to shout. *Look at me!* I shook my head in disbelief, shivering with pride. It can be done, I thought, still shaking my head as I headed home. I can do this for myself. I can do this by myself.

On my way home from the testing center, I stopped at the bakery around the corner from my house and bought a nine-inch strawberry shortcake. I had a one-person party, celebrating my score, standing at my kitchen counter and excavating chunks of cake with a chopstick and a spoon, bouncing on my feet, jabbing the air with the frosting-festooned chopstick, shouting, "I did it! I did it!" between giant mouthfuls. I gobbled the entire thing down to a pile of sticky crumbs, and it was delicious.

In the weeks that followed my test, I made it through work each day half-distracted as I mentally polished the lines of my personal essays for my graduate school applications. I selected and rejected words in order to most accurately describe the person I had now become. I applied to ten schools, but Harvard topped my list. "I will get accepted to Harvard," I repeated twice a day, forcing out those foolishly optimistic affirmations with confidence, as if I believed them.

If I could get into Harvard, I'd have a new label to carry for the rest of my life: Harvard student. I could let go of the others that had defined me: Fuckup. Former ultra-Orthodox Jew. If the universe would grant me this one little miracle, then I'd have the foundation for a normal life. A whole life. A life to be proud of.

In late February I received my first acceptance letter: University of California. Then Duke: no. Syracuse: yes, plus a hefty stipend. NYU: yes. Chicago: yes and a full scholarship.

The ache in my stomach did not dissolve. There was a placeholder in my future that only one school would fit. I needed this affirmation from the universe, that after so many failures and so much brokenness, I was worthy of a better life.

On a Friday in early March, I returned from work, exhausted and irritable. The stress of waiting to learn my fate was wearing on my nerves. I angrily picked at the stubborn knot on my belt until it loosened, pulled off my wrap dress, threw it in the general direction of my closet. I flipped open my laptop. An e-mail was waiting in my in-box. It had the word "Harvard" in the subject line.

I backed away from the computer. It's just a mailing-list thing, I thought. It's probably just a form letter. But not a no— don't let it be a no. Dear God-Universe-Everything-in-the-World, don't let it be a no. It's just a newsletter. Please. Please.

Holding my breath, I approached the computer again. In slow motion, I clicked on the e-mail.

"Dear Leah," it read. "We are pleased to offer you acceptance to Harvard University."

My legs gave out beneath me, and I sank to the floor. I rested my forehead in my palms, tasting the salty tears that ran over my lips as the word "Harvard" played over and over in my mind.

My mother had threatened to have me locked up, when, as a teenager, I had told her that I wanted to go to college. Lock me up as if I were a broken, wild animal, good for nothing. I had clung to the hope that, despite what my own mother thought of me, I still deserved a good life, even as I struggled to figure out what a good life was. And now I had Harvard on my side. Harvard. It felt like the largest stamp of secular approval in the world. Nobody could ever take that away from me. Nobody could ever again convince me that I was worthless.

On a Thursday night, a few weeks after my acceptance arrived, I sat on my bed with a container of sushi balanced on my knees. My laptop sat open on my pillow. I browsed Harvard's website, one hand clicking through descriptions of classes, the other balancing a slice of wasabi-smeared tuna between two chopsticks.

The phone rang.

It felt like weeks since the phone had rung. Wrong number, I thought, glancing at the caller ID. I didn't pick up. Five minutes later, it rang again.

"Hello?"

"Leah?"

It was a man's voice, vaguely familiar.

"Who's calling?"

"It's Mordy."

I froze. My little brother. I hadn't spoken to him in years. What should I say? I felt like an elephant facing a butterfly. One wrong move and he might disappear.

"How are you?" That felt safe enough.

"I'm okay."

What could I ask him next? I had so many questions. Where had he gotten my number? Why, after all this time, had he decided to reach out? Was there some problem in his religious or family situation? Was he looking for an ally? I had the urge to burst into a monologue about how I cared about him even if I didn't know him, but I thought that would be too hasty.

"Where are you calling from?" I asked.

"I'm in New York. I live here now."

Living here, New York.

"So you're not in yeshiva?" I was groping around in the dark, trying to figure out where my brother was. Who he was.

"I got kicked out," he said.

He's coming in my direction, I thought, visualizing him on a tightrope that led out of his community, toward me. The question was how to bring him closer without scaring him off. I knew how he must see me—how they all saw me, how they all saw anyone who left: Broken. Crazy. Dangerous. A zombie with outstretched arms, rabid for brains, souls. I ran through phrases in my mind. It would be easier in person.

"Do you want to meet?" I asked. "Talk about things?"

In the silence that followed, I felt the terror of losing him. A brother blowing full-sized into my life in an instant and then deflating, leaving a brother-sized hole where before there had been only a vague sense of loss. I rolled my eyes, frustrated with myself.

"That sounds like a good idea," he finally said.

We agreed to meet at a café near Union Square the following evening at seven. I arrived at 6:24 and ordered a mint tea. When it came, I wound the tea bag's string around my finger until it bit into my skin. I wondered what Mordy would look like. What this all meant. It was hard to believe that after losing my parents and siblings, I might finally get to have a brother. A permanent person in my life.

Thirty minutes later, Mordy walked in. I recognized him instantly, although the little boy I had known was now a man. He had the hooked Kaplan nose and warm Kaplan eyes and the same olive skin as me. We exchanged awkward hellos. He seemed like a stranger in the movement of his hands and the way he occupied his lean body. I scanned his clothing, looking for clues about his religious identity as he ordered a coffee from the waiter. He was wearing a white polo shirt and dark pants. His yarmulke was black velvet. Still religious, then. I smelled a whiff of cigarette smoke, a common yeshiva boy indulgence. My heart sank as I adjusted my expectations. He was probably just brashly curious. Probably had no intention of joining my new world. No desire to become a part of my life.

"Where do you live?" I asked.

"An apartment on Avenue M. A basement."

"It's so lovely to see you."

He smiled. Raised his eyebrows. Became my father for an instant in that familiar expression. It was uncanny.

"What are you up to these days?" I tried, as if we were old buddies who hadn't seen each other in a few months.

"I'm working," he said. "For a *kiruv* organization. For now."

Boys were supposed to learn in yeshiva, not work. But *kiruv*? That was the business of bringing secular Jews closer to Yeshivish Judaism. If he had failed as a yeshiva boy—too impatient to study for sixteen hours a day, too stubborn to bend to the strict dormitory rules—working for a *kiruv* organization allowed for a modicum of respectability. Ironically, proselytizing to secular

Jews was often undertaken by those unconventional in their own faith. But he'd said "for now." That sounded like an invitation.

"I'm actually going to Harvard next year," I said. I was pretty sure he would recognize the name of the university. As children, we hadn't known what "Ivy League" meant or the distinction between an undergraduate and graduate degree, but even we had heard of this ultimate secular school.

"Oh," he said. "How long are you going for?"

I could tell, deciphering his calm, polite response, that he thought I was going to visit.

"No, I mean I got into school there, to do an advanced degree, a master's degree."

He looked at me as if I had just told him I had been elected to serve as president of the United States. Confusion battled incredulity.

"Harvard? You?"

I could see in his shock all the things they had told him about me. How low his opinion of me was. The reminder of how my family thought of me was overwhelming.

"What about you?" I asked, changing the subject. Our new connection was too fragile for me to expose any more details of my life to him. "Are you thinking about going to college? Do you have a dream of doing something else?"

In the years since I had left the community, there had been a move toward allowing some college education. My parents did not support these compromises, but a few single-sex college programs had sprung up, providing sheltered environments in which religious men and women could get a four-year degree in practical subjects—accounting, computer programming, speech or occupational therapy.

"I don't know what I want to do," Mordy said. "I feel really lost when I think about it."

"Of course." I understood. I had felt as lost. If I hadn't had a piece of paper from the Harvard admissions office sitting on my desk, offering me a clear path forward into the future, I might still have felt as lost. There was only one life plan for Yeshivish children: learning for boys, and motherhood for girls. The dream-retarded brain was wretched at contorting itself to imagine other aspirations.

I couldn't tell how he felt about our conversation. He seemed wary. Resisting eye contact. Fiddling with his coffee cup. I was desperate to break through to him, to make sure he knew that I was there to help him if he wanted me to. I had to convince him that I was a friend.

"I have an idea," I said, draining my tea. "Come with me."

I paid the bill. He followed me outside and through the jostling crowds. We arrived at Barnes & Noble and rode the escalator up to the second floor, making small talk about Manhattan. He stopped at a table to look at a book about the Civil War.

"Wait here," I said. "I'll be back in a minute."

I headed to the newsstand section and plucked up magazines. *Motor Trend. Entrepreneur. SmartMoney. Bloomberg Markets. Architectural Digest. Dwell. Bon Appétit. Naval History. Horse & Rider. Spin. Mother Jones. Scientific American. Sports Illustrated. Macworld.* I filled my arms until the stack was almost too heavy to hold.

It was a thrill to offer Mordy this gesture of support. When I had begun my lonely struggles, I had so yearned to be swept off my feet with somebody's—anybody's—support. It filled me with joy to be doing for Mordy what had never been done for me.

Mordy was still reading the history book when I went to look for him. When he saw my arms laden with magazines, he looked at me quizzically.

"These are for you," I said, heading to a cashier so I could pay before he refused them. "I mean, of course, you're not going to like all of them, but maybe you'll find something here that's interesting. Who knows—maybe it'll be intriguing enough that you'll want to study it, maybe even make a career of it."

Magazines were carefully censored by the Yeshivish community. *Reader's Digest* was an acceptable vice. A *Rolling Stone* found under a pillow in a dormitory raid could get a boy kicked out of yeshiva. But if he was willing to talk with me, he was probably willing to read the magazines I was giving him.

"You're really sweet," he said, eyeing the stack. "But you don't have to do this."

"I want to."

I wanted to do anything to make his path easier than mine had been.

I wished I could hug him when we parted, a short while later, but I was afraid it might scare him. Already the conversation had died out. He held the Barnes & Noble bag tight against his chest.

"It was so nice to spend time with you," I said as we stood near the entrance to the subway. My heart ached again for my family. That pain had subsided with time, but looking into Mordy's face and seeing his familiar features had opened the wound. I hoped this meeting was a turning point. At least for the two of us.

"I hope we can talk again soon."

He offered a hesitant smile. "Yeah," he said. "Thanks. Have a good night."

In the days that followed, I waited for Mordy's call. It didn't come. My brother was not going to join me in my life. At least not yet. Eventually, he would go on his own journey of self-discovery, emerging as a secular man, a dear brother and ally, but it would take a few more years before I'd be sitting down to share a joyous lunch of bacon and eggs with him, his beautiful wife, and their adorable son.

I decided that in the few months I had left before going off to Harvard, I needed to learn to make friends. I had always been too busy juggling a double schedule of school and work to pursue friendships. I had a handful of acquaintances, but I felt, given my complicated history, that I didn't have enough in common with most people to bother investing in more. Instead, I had channeled my need for human connection into my relationships with men, always suffering a terrible loneliness.

But I had recently heard about Footsteps, a support group for former ultra-Orthodox Jews, and I decided it was about time for me to check it out. I would have to put aside my childhood prejudice against other people who had left religiosity, my assumption that they would all be stupid failures. I would have to bravely bring my whole self into the room, acknowledging my past along with my new hopes for my future. I would have to make myself vulnerable without the easy crutch of sex. I would have to. It was time.

The group met at the Fourteenth Street Y in downtown Manhattan. Chairs were arranged in a circle in the middle of a children's classroom, and a bottle of Coke and a package of chocolate chip cookies were laid out on a table. I found a seat and opened the book I had brought with me.

As people wandered in, I could see the aura of the past hovering around them. The men had short haircuts that suggested missing yarmulkes. The women were wrapped in bright, snug clothing, pairing jeans with heavy pearl necklaces I guessed they had received as gifts from their mothers-in-law when, at eighteen, they'd married.

I knew that I passed. I looked like a non-Jew in my jeans and ragged sweater, my hair cut short, curling in jaunty tufts around my head.

The meeting was led by a social worker, who orchestrated a conversation about our struggles in our old worlds and our new worlds.

"I went home to my family in Williamsburg," one woman said. "I have my life, right, I'm a grown-up, I pay my rent, go to college, but suddenly, in my parents' home, I felt like a child again. They sneer at me, and I just—I lose all of my sense of self-worth."

Remembering my last trip home, I knew exactly what she meant.

"I need to get jeans," one guy said. "I decided I'm done with the black pants every day. But I feel silly walking into a store. I don't even know how to buy jeans! How does one buy jeans?"

We laughed at his mock outrage, and I felt a cathartic release in remembering my traumatizing experience trying to buy a thong, years ago.

As I listened to the stories, my eyes roved the room. I was shocked that these people, so similar to me, had been coexisting in New York all this time, while I'd thought I was alone. The feeling of belonging was foreign and a little bit frightening, but I could not quell my amazement.

My eyes kept returning to the young man who sat across from me, his legs stretched indolently in front of him. He was short, broadly built, with thick blond hair and inquisitive blue eyes that were fixed on me for most of the session. His name was Zeke. Something about this Zeke looked deeply familiar, although I knew I had never met him before. I tried to figure out where I had seen him, but I came up blank.

"Hi," he said to me when the session ended. "What train are you taking home?"

"The Q," I told him.

"Me too. I'll come with you."

I smiled at his abruptness and his boldness, the assumption that this would be okay with me.

Zeke was three years younger than me. On the train, he slouched in the orange seat as we chatted about our families. He'd been raised in a Hasidic home in Borough Park. I could help him, I thought, recognizing echoes of myself in his ambition, his hunger to rebuild himself. Maybe we'll become friends.

Perhaps because I was older than him, I felt confident in his presence. He seemed to be a different species of man than any I had ever met. He bore vestiges of a religious past in his intensity, but he was freedom-loving and progressive in his views: singing the praises of his tattooed gay socialist professor, insisting that atheism was the only option for a true intellectual, explaining Nietzsche's ideas with the focus of a yeshiva boy parsing a complex Talmudic text. I enjoyed the awed look in his eyes when I told him about Harvard. I relished the strength in my voice when I talked to him.

Zeke and I saw each other again, taking the train to a café in Union Square, sharing more of our histories, some of our secrets. In the days that followed, our friendship grew into countless phone calls and e-mails.

One Sunday in May, we decided to buy bikes together. We found a guy selling two of them on Craigslist and rode the train to Chinatown to pick them up.

"I haven't ridden in years," Zeke admitted as we rolled them away.

"Think you still can?" I teased, swinging my leg over the seat and pushing forward. "Think you can keep up?"

I took off into the chilly air, my legs alive as I soared down the block. Zeke pedaled frantically until he pulled ahead of me.

"Who's keeping up now?" he shouted, flying across an intersection. I chased after him, and we swallowed up the city blocks, looking over our shoulders to keep track of the impatient cars and each other.

He stopped in front of city hall, got off his bike, and kneeled down beside it.

"What's up?" I asked, slamming on my brakes and dismounting. "Everything okay?"

His fingers were black with grease as he showed me the two pieces of his broken bike chain.

"No wonder the bike was so cheap," he said, laughing. He wasn't upset. It was a relief to be around a guy who was so carefree, who didn't move with a fragile dignity that I always needed to be on my toes to protect. We walked our bikes at our sides and bumped them down the subway stairs to take the train home.

"I think I figured it out," I said as the train rattled over the bridge.

"What?"

"Who you look like. You've always looked familiar to me, and now I think I know why. I'll show you when we get back to my place."

When we got in, I opened my laptop and Googled *Kidnapped*, finding the version of the movie I had watched as a child, years and lifetimes ago. There on the screen was the actor James MacArthur. I knew him as Davie, the first man I had ever dreamed of marrying. His square jaw, blue eyes, round-tipped nose, and blond curls were identical to Zeke's. Small world, I thought. What a funny coincidence. I told Zeke about Davie, and how I used to guiltily fantasize about this movie actor wanting to marry me.

"Breaking the rules, even then," Zeke said, and I laughed in agreement. Being able to laugh with someone who understood my journey made the whole experience that much lighter to bear. With his friendship, I was released from the intensity of my mind, where I had endlessly rehashed my life, blaming myself for all that had happened. I saw that my journey was not that different from the path others took—that life was tough but I was strong, and I was not alone.

In the fall I started graduate school, and Zeke drove up to Massachusetts every weekend to be with me. He encouraged me to track down Blaze, the roommate I had married and abandoned, and to file for divorce. Not long after the papers were finalized,

Zeke and I married. We had a beautiful child together, born on October 2, Gandhi's birthday. Gandhi, the one who had reassured me years before that I would, indeed, have children.

But before all that joy, I would have my own simple, happy ending, alone.

On my last day in New York, I wore my new crimson Harvard T-shirt and a pair of denim shorts, with my hair pulled into a messy bun, as I packed up my apartment, pulling my pictures down, leaving chips of paint on the wall. I had already thrown out bags of trash: modest dresses I hadn't worn in years, an unopened box of baking powder from when I'd once been overcome by an ephemeral desire to bake, stained sheets I'd found balled in the back of the closet.

Everything else I owned sat in a small heap in the middle of the bedroom. A late-summer thunderstorm boomed across the sky as I kneeled on the dusty floor, squeezing books into a cardboard box. What do grad students wear, I wondered, rolling mismatched socks together. I hope I don't stick out like a sore thumb. Like a nerd. At Harvard. *Haaar-varrrrd*. The word still sang in my mind.

I had thrown out stacks of old tax returns and college papers, but I carefully packed every one of my acceptance letters. The most important one was secured in a cardboard folder and buried at the bottom of my battered suitcase.

This was the same suitcase I had pulled out of a pile in my parents' basement lifetimes ago. A subdued teenage girl in a long blue skirt, I'd been so eager to begin my adventures in Manchester. I had proudly crossed out Goldy's name and printed "Leah Kaplan" across the side of the case. At some point in the years since, I had struck through "Kaplan" and written "Vincent" above it in block letters. "What a trip it's been," I said aloud. "What a trip we've been on, down to the bottom. And now we travel again, old friend." I gave the dusty side a friendly slap. "Onward and upward."

Plopping down on the suitcase, I jammed it shut, reaching

around my legs to yank the zipper closed. Cracks of lightning flashed through the tawny air. I rested in the middle of my empty apartment, inhaling the scent of lemon-based cleaner, watching the rain run down the dusty window, savoring the stillness of the last minutes before I moved on.

afterword

Frankly, I'd love
a better word than sad right now. Something less drowsy
and inert, something to reflect the woman you were drowning
in her bathtub, clutching a martini. The Amazon's
sheared off breast perhaps, or the war cries that rattled their jungle
like silver spears.

—PAISLEY REKDAL, *Canzone*

EARLY ONE APRIL MORNING IN 2010, I cupped a mug of tea in my hands and stood at the window of my Washington, D.C., apartment, looking out at my world. I was six blocks from the White House, four blocks from the office where I managed an antipoverty program for a philanthropic network and three and a half hours from Zeke's apartment in New Jersey, where he and I alternated weekends.

Here I am, I thought, taking in the cherry blossoms bursting forth like popcorn on the trees below. This is my wonderland.

It seemed like a miracle, but I had finally managed to create what felt like a "normal" secular life. There were no indicators of trauma in my brisk and cheerful days. There were no clumsy remnants of ultra-Orthodoxy in my conversation. That past of poverty, blood, and shame belonged to a different woman, a woman whom I rarely thought of. After one brutal Washington winter, I felt I had earned my citizenship in this city. I was sure I'd be here for a long time.

I had finally arrived.

In the narrative of my journey, I had thought the moment of "arrival" would be at the start of graduate school, almost three years before, but that time was too marked with growing pains to offer the sense of achievement I sought.

I spent my first year at Harvard ripping my gaze away from my classmates' faces. They all appeared to radiate some magnetic aura. Was it privilege? Intelligence? Confidence? They seemed to be encased in a smooth skin that I didn't have. My hair was too frizzy. My jeans were too baggy and frayed. In introductions, I flailed into scattered divulgences about my origins, watching helplessly as my classmates backed away, their discomfort masked in tight smiles and arm's-length curiosity. In class, when we debated the ethics of imposing feminism on fundamentalist Islamic women, people volleyed arguments referencing work assignments in Mogadishu, tours of duty in Kabul, and political theories that I had never heard of. I threw my arm up, exploding, when called upon, in a tear-tinged tirade of what secular life could take away from women who derived meaning from their restrictive faith. My outburst was met with startled silence, as if I had burped loudly in a quiet church.

Intimidated by the mysterious procedures of casual conversation that I had never mastered, I stayed home in the evenings while my classmates went out together and grew thickets of friendship that made them seem that much more impenetrable to me.

My social ineptitude aside, Harvard was a paradise of opportunity. I traveled to Sierra Leone to explore their criminal justice system. I worked on municipal food systems for the city of Boston. I learned powerful theories of social change with my new guru, the extraordinary Dr. Ronnie Heifetz. Slowly, I picked out a few precious friendships, mostly with older students. As I began to see glimpses of people's private lives, I realized that my self-pity had blinded me. I was not the only one with a story.

In my second year, I packed my zebra-print leggings away and began to blend into the herd of khaki. By the time graduation arrived, my history had faded and I had absorbed most of the rules of my new culture. When I arrived in Washington, I was no longer Leah Vincent, former ultra-Orthodox Jew. I was Leah Vincent, Harvard graduate.

And so on that spring day, as I finished my tea, rinsed my mug in the sink, and set off to work, I continued to relish the awe I felt, at the life I was now fortunate enough to live.

When I got to my office, I twirled open the blinds and dove in: e-mails to academics studying homelessness in California, research on metrics for measuring after-school program success, and a meeting with my colleagues to brainstorm themes for the regional conferences that I would produce over the next two years.

At three, I rolled my chair back from my desk and pulled a peanut butter sandwich from my bag. Taking quick bites, I logged into my personal e-mail. There I found a message from a formerly ultra-Orthodox friend back in New York. It was about Tammy Silverman, an acquaintance with wheat blonde hair and a smile that never reached her eyes.

Tammy was dead. She had committed suicide.

I placed the remnants of my sandwich carefully on my desk and read the e-mail again. I read it again after that, and then once more, as if, had I only paid enough attention, the words would fall open and come to mean something else other than what they did.

As the letters blurred on the screen, the contrast between

where I stood and where Tammy lay hit me hard. I saw myself in Tammy. Saw the end that by all rights should have been mine. I looked down the path that had brought me to this office, in this city, with that maroon framed graduate degree hanging on the wall. I traced my evolution back to that girl with bloodstained arms and empty belly, pinned beneath a man's body, and back before that, to that voiceless child, heart brimming with trust and faith, oblivious to the precipice crumbling beneath her feet.

Exhaustion seeped into my limbs. I curled up on the chair, the taste of peanut butter now rancid in my mouth. Laying my heavy head on my knees, I closed my eyes.

"I've been so focused on trying to prove myself," I said to Zeke that evening. "Prove to who? The world? My parents? I can't do this anymore. I need to face myself. I need to tell my story. I need to write my memoir."

"Why don't you come live with me?" he asked. "You can move in and just write."

Zeke and I had known each other for three years by then, and we had been in a long-distance relationship for almost all of that time. We were fully committed to each other, and our lives were deeply intertwined, but first my school and then our jobs kept us in different states. Zeke's offer meant that not only would he share his home with me, he would also bear the burden of supporting us both.

"You're up for that?" I asked.

"This is important," he said. "You need to tell this story. I want to help you do this."

I quit my job, moved in with Zeke, and began to write, sorting through boxes of diaries, photos, poems, and letters. I was committed to recounting this story without the censor of shame, and I wrote bluntly about my own mistakes and the mistakes of others when they were relevant to my experiences. I had no interest in writing an exposé of ultra-Orthodoxy or of my family. If I had, I would have written an entirely different book. I wanted to bear witness only to my own experiences. In my writing, I used the voice of the girl in the story without the overlay of my current perceptions. I wanted to tell her story that happened then, not mine, now.

As complexities in one area of life often inspire complexities in others and adventures often beget adventures, I have many stories to tell. But while an autobiography attempts to catalog all of a person's years, this was a memoir, and like any other, it dove into one narrative and attempted to capture that fully.

Four days before my thirty-first birthday, I accepted a publisher's offer for *Cut Me Loose*. In response to Tammy, in response to my own ghosts, I would fulfill that promise I had made to myself so many years earlier—that if I survived, I would tell my story to the world.

When I began my journey out of ultra-Orthodoxy as a teenager, I made no effort to hunt down other formerly ultra-Orthodox Jews scattered across the vast secular world. I didn't question what I had been taught—that my peers would be disgusting, miserable failures. But over the past ten years it has become easier to confront that myth as the advent of the Internet and the founding of Footsteps (a nonprofit serving people leaving ultra-Orthodoxy for a self-determined life) led to the rise of a vibrant community of self-identified formerly ultra-Orthodox Jews. Members of this community often called themselves OTD, for Off the *Derech* (path), a reappropriated ultra-Orthodox pejorative.

This blossoming OTD community was based in New York, and as I worked on my book I began to attend more OTD events. Each encounter fed a growing sense of relief. These were people with whom I could finally be my full-faceted self. They spoke the exotic language of both my childhood and my transitional experiences. And what people! Courageous, strong, creative, funny, and kind. I was flattered and grateful to be accepted by them.

The OTD community has a fierce commitment to self-expression and social justice, and it has developed advocacy initiatives to address the plethora of crises that our communities of origin have swept under the rug.

Some ultra-Orthodox rabbis shield pedophilic predators from criminal investigations while telling children who have been molested to keep their mouths shut and forget what happened. Members of the OTD community organized protests and garnered international media attention that began to slowly shift the paradigm of how sex abuse is handled.

When people try to leave ultra-Orthodoxy for a self-determined life, they often struggle under the heavy prophecy constantly impressed upon them that, having left their faith, their only possible future is drug addiction, prostitution, and death. Members of the OTD community developed online communities and in-person meet-up groups to support each other and created a project called It Gets Besser (*besser*, Yiddish for "better") that showcases OTD success stories to counter that myth of failure.

Many ultra-Orthodox boys' schools offer almost no math or science, and when the state and local government refused to enforce children's rights to a basic education, members of the OTD community campaigned to raise awareness about this issue and to encourage ultra-Orthodox parents to advocate for their children's learning.

Many ultra-Orthodox women are trapped in a web of shame and threats that deprives them of the right to be equal members of their households, communities, and society, so members of the OTD community collected and disseminated information on women's subjugation and objectification through the laws of ultra-Orthodox "modesty" and began to engage rabbis to address these issues.

In many ultra-Orthodox communities, girls and boys move swiftly from childhood into arranged marriages and then (with birth control largely forbidden) large families of their own. By the time a moment of consciousness has the opportunity to dawn and a longing for a college education, personal autonomy, or the experience of romantic love can begin to develop, a young man or woman in their early twenties can find themselves with a spouse and three or four children. Not only must this individual now learn how to navigate out into a self-determined life, in the almost inevitable divorce that follows, they must also often battle an organized response by their religious community that will rally financial, legal, emotional, and practical support to ensure the religious spouse receives custody of that person's children.

For many ultra-Orthodox Jews, anything is allowed and everything is encouraged to do what it takes to ensure these young Jewish souls are "saved" from the "corrupting" influence of a parent who might not only model forbidden behavior but also encourage their daughter to dream of a professional career or seek to move their son into a more moderate Jewish or secular school that provides a full and violence-free education.

Rabbis, former friends, and even a person's own parents will sometimes take the stand to testify that the person seeking a self-determined life is mentally unstable and thus a dangerously unfit parent. Psychologists who make their living serving an ultra-Orthodox clientele will testify that it is healthier to alienate a child from her parent rather than allow the grave damage of "confusing" that child with exposure to a father who doesn't wear a skullcap or a mother who wears jeans. This astounding evaluation of children's needs is now encoded as legal precedent in New York.

The parent seeking a self-determined life, who has often just lost her home, her friends, and her job, can be subject to intense bullying, manipulation, and threats from the authorities of her community as she sinks into astronomical debt in a struggle to defend herself from the high-powered lawyer bankrolled for her ex, until the family court judges (who are sometimes elected with the bloc ultra-Orthodox vote) extract the price of freedom: custody of the children awarded to the religious parent.

Outraged by this injustice, members of the OTD community offered funds, company to court dates, a listening ear, babysitting, and connections to legal resources to parents facing this daunting communal opponent in their fight for their children. As the scope of the need became more apparent, members of the OTD community organized to develop a program at Footsteps that now provides full case management and legal representation for parents choosing a self-determined life.

I was fortunate enough to work on a few of these projects, while many more were developed and made successful by others in the OTD community. I am constantly awed by the commitment that my peers have to help others despite the overwhelming challenges and losses many of them must face in their own lives.

Beyond these problems within ultra-Orthodoxy, there is much that is beautiful and valuable about that community, and there are many wonderful ultra-Orthodox people. Perhaps it is only a small minority of people who are responsible for these moral failures. But while the ultra-Orthodox community is generally so vigilant about perceived violations of the laws of modesty that a small wave of wigs of risqué length can trigger campaigns and conferences to address the crisis, there has been no such response to address the immodesty of grown men putting their hands on the bodies of young boys or teenage girls.

The ultra-Orthodox community holds other Jewish communities responsible for perceived moral failure in politics, religion, or society, but there has been little of that accountability between ultra-Orthodox groups. When one ultra-Orthodox subsect recently threatened, slandered, and shunned a young woman bold enough to pursue justice after being molested by a rabbi, and then held a large fund-raiser for the accused rabbi's legal defense, there was no public outcry from other ultra-Orthodox leaders.

I became involved in these projects because human rights

were at stake, because a group claiming absolute moral superiority should be held to a high standard of ethical behavior, because freedom in the United States of America should not come with the price tag that I and many of my OTD friends had to pay, because the ultra-Orthodox leaders who should be addressing these issues are persistently ignoring them while few outsiders seem to understand or care enough to hold them accountable. But, most of all, I spoke out because while I did have a lot of anger due to my experiences, I also treasured a deep affection for my community of origin. I didn't want to see it rot away. I respected its strength enough to hope that if its members were no longer allowed to turn their backs on these problems, ultra-Orthodoxy might flourish as a healthy and moral way of life.

After *Cut Me Loose* was published, I anticipated backlash from the ultra-Orthodox community, but it was not as bad as I had expected. One publication compared my memoir to the Holocaust-era Nazi newspaper *Der Sturmer*, and a number of rabbis and Internet commenters declared me crazy.

I am not sure what "crazy" means, other than "I want an excuse to silence you and not have to engage with the substance of the issues you raise," but if it purports to be a commentary on my mental health, my memoir unabashedly describes my struggles with self-harm, my stay on a psychiatric ward, and my engaging in risky behavior. Those were defining components of my younger years and defining elements of this book. I was a naive adolescent when I went through what I did. I made poor choices as I reacted to the harsh and unforgiving realities that I encountered.

If "crazy" is a commentary on my current life, my life will never be "normal" by my parents' standard or by the standards of a nice middle-aged Evangelical Republican couple in Wichita, Kansas. I hold a deeply traumatic past, and my current work as a writer focuses on examining taboo realities many "normal" people have no interest in. My life is irreverent and bold, and it contains a fair share of scars, but it is also healthy.

But, more important, even if I did have a mental illness, why would that mean that I was incapable of expressing my reality—a reality that others have also experienced and talked about? And what messages are being conveyed to oneself and to one's audience when those who dissent are labeled "crazy"?

What, I wonder, would I or any other person who has a traumatic experience leaving ultra-Orthodoxy have to do to be given "permission" to recount his or her experiences without being attacked in this way?

In addition to diagnosing my mental health, people also offered stories of their own experiences with my family as proof that my recounting of my life was a lie. I spent a lot of time in her house, many people said. Her father is the most gentle, welcoming, and open-minded rabbi. He would never do these things she describes.

My father has devoted his life to persuading other Jews to accept his Yeshivish lifestyle, and he is indeed often forgiving and patient and nonjudgmental with his congregants and students as they move toward embracing his values.

When I began doing interviews in the months before my book was published, my father issued a statement to the media:

"Regarding her teenage years, it is clear to me that she does not, or perhaps is not always able to, separate her imaginings from the facts. Leah first came under the care of a psychiatrist when she was thirteen, and over the years she was in treatment for serious disorders and self-destructive behaviors. As painful as the situation is to our family, we hope that her gaining the media attention she has craved for so long will bring her some measure of peace. We will continue to love her, always."

He is a well-spoken man.

I encountered this statement for the first time on the night before I was to appear on Katie Couric's TV show. The producer called me, alarmed. Despite the weeks she and I had spent talking and preparing for the episode, she had just received this statement from my father and now wondered, if, indeed, she was about to put a schizophrenic pathological liar on the show.

I connected the producer with my brother.

"I fully corroborate Leah's story," Martin told her in a statement. "I vividly recall the years during which she was first sent away from home for not abiding by the religious rules of our home and subsequently vilified and ostracized as she pursued her goals, unsanctioned by our family's religious values. . . .

"My parents would constantly scorn Leah, informing us she had been gripped by mental insanity, by satanic forces (in Hebrew: *yetzer hara*), and physical impurity through contact with gentile men.

"Years later, when I went through my own journey, leaving the ultra-Orthodox community to pursue my goals, I discovered that Leah was in fact a successful woman who was ostracized for not adhering to the rules of our community. . . . I was to discover that she is a wonderful sister as well."

My father has never allowed me to tell him what happened in those years when I was on my own. He has never allowed me to explain how his choices affected my life. He has never allowed me to describe how I interpreted his choices at the time, in my new context. We have revived our relationship two or three times over the past ten years, and each time I try to move to this essential conversation, the fragile threads of connection are broken by a sudden, absolute silence, and again I am an orphan.

Of course, even if he was willing to sit down with compassionate eyes and ask me to share with him my story, the whole story, what you have read and all the messy bits, unruly details, and other story lines that were not included in this single narrative, my memories of my relationship with my father would not match his memories of his relationship with me. How could it? We observed our interactions from different viewpoints.

He saw me.

I saw him.

He was a middle-aged Yeshivish rabbi, and I was one of his eleven children.

I was a teenage Yeshivish girl, and he was my holy father.

My father is a good man. He made poor choices in parenting me, choices that, for whatever reason, he could not bring himself to abandon. And me? I am a good woman, but I have certainly made mistakes with the people whom I love. I have displayed my own bullheaded obstinacy. I do not think he is wholly bad and I am wholly good.

Despite my offenses of choosing a self-determined life and sharing my story publically, I have never stopped loving my father. I have never stopped hoping that one day we will reconcile.

In addition to my father's statement, there was one other bit of feedback that stood out in the swirl of publicity after publishing *Cut Me Loose*.

"Why does she always talk about being raped," one ultra-Orthodox rabbi asked, peeved. "Her obsession with it is unhealthy."

I do talk about being raped a lot. Every speech and almost every interview I have given since my book was published contains some variation of these three words: "I was raped."

For the first thirty-one years of my life, I never said those words publically. Because of how I was raised, I never considered myself a victim of rape, although I was, in the encounter with Nicholas that I describe in this book, and in another encounter with someone else that is not recounted here.

My mouth goes dry every time I look for those three words.

I hate having to boil down that experience into one manageable sentence.

I hate having to deposit that moment into this moment.

Each "I was raped" feels like it travels through my sternum, producing a small crack in the shell of bone, muscle, and flesh as it exits me, so that by now my chest is lined with a network of hairline fractures. I am afraid, one day, an "I was raped" will break from me, and with the force of its exit, the entire fissured surface of my chest will crumple, and I will collapse in on myself.

When I wrote *Cut Me Loose*, I was inspired by the words of the poet Muriel Rukeyser:

"What would happen if one woman told the truth about her life? The world would split open."

Then, those lines seemed a testament to the size and power of women's true lives. Now I wonder: Whose world, exactly, is being split open? And is it split like an egg shattering to release a chick, or is it split like the earth's crust cracking apart to release a teeming mass of lava that swallows all the life in its path?

Still, I am going to continue saying those three words. I am going to say "I was raped" a hundred times. I am going to say "I was raped" a thousand times. I am going to say "I was raped" ten thousand times. I am going to say "I was raped" for every girl and woman who isn't allowed to say it. Doesn't know she can. Is punished if she does. I'm going to keep on disturbing people by saying "I was raped" until they are more offended by the act of rape than the words that recount it.

After *Cut Me Loose* was published, an OTD friend told me that she had heard too many stories like mine in our community, and she wanted to do something about it. We began to gather data in an informal survey to find out how many women in our OTD community had experienced sexual assault. We discovered rates almost double those of the general population. Most of the experiences of sexual assault or rape had happened as these women were on their journeys of transition into the secular world.

"I barely knew what sex was," one woman told me.

"I didn't know I was allowed to say no," said another.

I heard from women from many different communities, religious and secular, who told me that they had experienced sexual trauma similar to what I describe. Our modern world has a crisis around female sexuality, sexual expression, and sexual safety, and I'm not sure that any ideological group fully understands the problem or the solution.

So I will keep on saying "I was raped" until enough people say "I was raped," and the conversation that has not happened, or not happened loud enough, or with enough people, happens, until women with young sons worry as much about their sons one day becoming rapists, as I worry about my daughter one day being raped, until no mothers have to worry about this at all.

It is a beautiful Tuesday afternoon. I am sitting on my pink swivel chair in a T-shirt and cutoff jeans, my curly hair loose, and a glass of tea and a pile of dried mango beside me on my desk. The fan murmurs at my back, my fingertips click on my laptop, and Leonard Cohen croons his love over the sound system.

My daughter is with her nanny at the park down the block, looking for music to dance to, but she came in earlier, blue eyes shining, to announce that she had learned a song with the other *kindawach* at yoga. She sang it to me:

"My liddle light bows to yow liddle light, youw liddle light bows to my liddle light, *mamasday*!"

Kindawach is her lisping Yiddish for "children," *mamasday* is her attempt at the Sanskrit for "I bow to the divine in you," and she, my patchwork child—along with her father, my brother, our OTD friends, and perhaps, in some ways, many people of all backgrounds around the globe—is my companion on this adventure navigating a world that is never quite what we signed up for, never quite the way we want it, and yet still gorgeous in its perfect imperfections.

Down on my inner arms, I see my second and third tattoos: two small squares, the purple of a fresh fig, one placed midway up my inner right arm, the other an inch higher on my left. I didn't want the squares to line up exactly. Life doesn't exist lined up. It exists in the tension of the gap between what is and what we want, one forever striving to catch up with the other.

In the stories I shared in *Cut Me Loose*, I composed a single arc of struggle to redemption. But looking back from where I am now, I can see that there is no Messiah, no unrelenting happily ever after. There are battles, hunts, and quests that end in triumph or failure, then periods of rest, and more battles, hunts, and quests—the size of our dragons keeping pace with our growing strength.

My new tattoos are in honor of my two goddesses: Hope in endless darkness and Humiliation, the price for following that hope, the wings that have carried me this far, that carry me still.

Hope is prettier than Humiliation, but it's a measly brain without a body, imagining destinations yet incapable of reaching them. Hope dreams outrageous dreams because it's indifferent to the costs of making them come true. Humiliation is the golem that must lurch to life to do hope's bidding.

Till you get to the bar you also need a drink, says the old Yiddish expression. Till you become empowered, you need power to get there. Humiliation can be that power: Proposing a grandiose project that is laughed down, so you learn how to present it more effectively the next time. Walking away from the end of a relationship with the humiliation of an exposed heart, but knowing that your heart is stronger than ever. Publishing a bold essay that is roundly criticized but, in the process, opens a new conversation. Recording your most difficult truths in a book that is rejected over and over again, until you gather enough uncomfortable criticism to improve it and win that book contract.

When I was applying to graduate schools, someone I had respected laughed at my presumption when I told him I was going to try for Harvard. I was so ashamed in that moment and in the weeks after, as I ruminated on it. But if I wasn't willing to risk the humiliation of failure, the humiliation of presumption, I would have never earned the graduate degree now sitting on my shelf.

Of course, Humiliation doesn't always give good returns. It's like radiation: it harms you every time, but sometimes, if you're very lucky, it will also save you. Neither of my goddesses is beautiful—even Hope, so venerated, for me, is a parasite. Feeding on me, it wants me as large and fat as possible, so it sends me out on big humiliating missions that will stretch me as far as I can go without killing me. It's an evolutionary cycle, with Hope infecting me with larger and larger doses of hope, sending me out on ever more humiliating journeys that push me further, make me more, so Hope can ask for more than that the next time.

This isn't an elegant journey, but it's one that I love, one that has created a beautiful, anguished, vibrant, meaningful life that I treasure.

Sometimes I think back to that moment in 2010 when I chose to leave the "normal" life I was finally putting the last touches on, to instead try to create this freewheeling life of adventure and self-expression. Sometimes I wonder if I chose to leave my successful career and assimilated identity because I was afraid of having finally gotten what I had always wanted, so afraid, I had to abandon it. But other times I think about the three-alarm fire that consumed the apartment next door to mine, weeks after I moved out of Washington, D.C., and I wonder if the black frame of soot that marked the window that I used to love to dawdle at in the mornings was some kind of somber omen for the life that awaited me had I stayed there, and I am overwhelmed with relief and gratitude that I had the courage to make the choice that I did and the love from Zeke to follow through, to bring myself here, in this particular life.

With gratitude to you and to all my readers and to my true friends, my mighty teachers, my holy mentors, and my chosen family, I leave you here until next time.

Have hope. Use humiliation. Speak your own truths.

Leah Vincent
New York City
August 2014

acknowledgments

My deep gratitude to all who have helped bring this book to life, especially Anouk Markovits, whose faith and generosity revived me when I had given up; Shulem Deen, who, with wisdom and compassion, coached me in the creation of this book; Jesse Miller, for his precious encouragement and support; Samuel (Ushy) Katz, for his profound insight and for being my sounding board; all my friends in the OTD community, for inspiring me with their courage and strengthening me with their love; Jessica Kaufman, for giving me the peace to write; Danni Michaeli, for helping me hold on to the dream; Adam Eaglin, for being my gracious and wise partner in birthing this project; Ronit Feldman, for her phenomenal clarity and invigorating kindness; Nan Talese and the entire team at Nan A. Talese/Doubleday, for all their assistance; Phin, for holding my hand every single day of this bumpy journey and for giving me the best compliment I have ever received on my writing; and my beloved Hope and Humiliation, who have always carried me through.